# A Kid's Guide
## to the **Louvre**
### for **Adults**

*For Claude Courant, who loves the Louvre,*
*which loves him in return.*

*Special thanks to Laurence Golstenne*
*whose pertinent and impertinent remarks*
*have contributed to the enrichment and structure*
*of this book.*

A Kid's Guide to the Louvre for Adults
is also available in French under the title
*Comment parler du Louvre aux enfants.*

Front cover: *Mona Lisa*, detail

© 2005, Le Baron Perché
28, rue de Sévigné
75004 Paris

ISBN : 2-35131-007-1
Dépôt légal : octobre 2005
Imprimé en France

# A Kid's Guide to the Louvre for Adults

◆Isabelle Bonithon Courant

Translated by Carine Thévenet & Lamar Hawkins

The first
series of books
for kids'sake...
aimed
at grown-ups

Le baron perché

# table of contents

# Foreward

The Louvre museum has become a site not-to-be-missed. Today, some six million visitors crowd through its gates each year, all prepared to tackle thousands of art works exhibited throughout kilometers of galleries, sometimes doing all this only to see —for at least once in their lives—a masterpiece such as the *Mona Lisa*. We take for granted the existence of masterpieces without ever wondering what the word stands for. At the end of the day, what exactly is a masterpiece?

The Louvre was the first museum created in France to open its doors to the public. It is, in itself, an exaggeration of the concept of museum, by its gigantic scale and encyclopedic character. Yet, who today remembers the origins of the word museum? Why were museums created and what is their purpose?

The Louvre is the inevitable museum stop when on a trip to Paris, both for the wealth of its holdings and its fame. Nevertheless, it remains a slightly intimidating place for adults, and all the more so for children. How should you approach such an imposing place with children? How best visit the Louvre without putting them off and tiring of it yourself? What can you show children and how can you help them observe a Greek sculpture or an ivory work from the Middle Ages?

Better understanding the genesis of a place such as the Louvre, is one way of learning to make the most of your visit. This book is not meant to be an exhaustive guide, but rather an aid in helping you better understand the museum's story and riches, as well as its constraints. It offers a certain amount of historical information in addition to practical advice that will help you visit the Louvre serenely. Finally, a selection of thirty-one works of art will give you tips on how to enhance your observation of art or archeological objects. These selected works come from eight of the Louvre's nine departments—excluding the Department of Arts and Civilizations of Africa, Asia, Oceania and the Americas, to be located in a future branch museum, Quai Branly.

# What is a ??? mas ??.

erpiece?

## On the difficulty of appreciating masterpieces

"She's so small." "She's all yellow." "I can't see her..."
Be on the lookout—tricky situation ahead. One day we all risk finding ourselves
unsettled by a child's disappointment upon viewing *Mona Lisa*; we may fall short
of an explanation to justify the long journey—and sometimes the long wait—required
to access the masterpiece of all masterpieces. We may even share the child's
thoughts without daring to admit them.
Indeed, nothing is more obscure and disconcerting than the notion of "masterpiece."
It is a notion that does not only concern the emotional, sentimental or personal
relationship we have with the piece, but also applies to the sharing of a collective
opinion that we sometimes find difficult to grasp.
If a child's enthusiasm is spontaneous, so too are his or her deceptions. The obstacle
course that is imposed, in order to contemplate some of the Louvre's masterpieces,
will be all the more puzzling for a child if we are unable to justify the universal
impact of these outstanding works.
Therefore, in order to be better prepared to face the barrage of questions
that children ask innocently, why don't we just return to the source? Why not try
to understand the difficult and sometimes random path taken by a work of art
in becoming a masterpiece?

## The masterpiece paradox

A masterpiece is a work of art we must absolutely see, solely because of its fame.
Can you imagine going to the Louvre and not seeing the *Mona Lisa* or the *Venus de
Milo*? Inconceivable! However, we rarely ask ourselves about the origins of this
celebrity. By the way, are all masterpieces famous? Nothing is less certain.
In general better known than other works of art, masterpieces are not necessarily
the easiest to comprehend; hence, not necessarily the easiest to teach how or why
they should be appreciated. Visiting a museum by only viewing its masterpieces
is an attempt to understand that which is the most complex and difficult to grasp.

## When did we begin using the term masterpiece?

In the Middle Ages, the word *masterpiece* qualified a work executed by an artisan
—a journeyman—in order to obtain his master's degree, which is to say, the right
to practice his art independently. Often intricate, the masterpiece ("master's piece")
attested the virtuosity and technical skill acquired by the artisan during
his apprenticeship.
Depending on the craft, this work—a model, a piece of furniture, a framework,
a staircase—was proof that the artisan had reached the maturity from which ensued
his independence as a journeyman.

Some of these masterpieces—mostly from the 18th and 19th centuries since the oldest pieces have not been preserved—can be seen today in the Musées du Compagnonnage (workers' guilds museums) in Tours or in Troyes. This artisan tradition lives on to this day.

## Did painters and sculptors also have to execute a masterpiece?

Yes... In the 17th and 18th centuries, young artists were required to execute a "master's piece" in order to enter the "Academy" (the society of artists in service to the court which encouraged the spread of a particular teaching style). Joining the Academy allowed an artist to begin a career working for the kingdom's great aristocrats. In this way, an evaluation was made of the young artist's capacity to respect certain rules (mastery of perspective, anatomical drawing, proportions; knowledge of the Greco-Roman literary and artistic rules...). Morceaux de reception, or reception pieces, is how the Academy called specific masterpieces created by painters and sculptors. Some of these reception pieces are preserved at the Louvre.

## Did all masterpieces follow the criteria decreed by the Academy?

Antoine Watteau, with the *Pilgrimage to Cythera*, proposed a reception piece based on a topic derived from contemporary theater, which at the time had never been used in painting—the *Fête Galante* (a topic evoking the game of seduction). He imposed a new set of themes that were added to those already accepted by the Academy (historical painting, portrait, genre scenes, landscape, still-life). His painting attained considerable success in the 18th century, later inspiring Paul Verlaine's anthology entitled *Fêtes Galantes*.
As for Chardin, he obtained unanimous recognition with *The Skate*, despite having chosen to work in the minor genre of still-life, which was not highly valued by the academicians. Praised by Diderot, studied by Paul Cézanne, the painting now hangs on its own wall, consecrating its status as a masterpiece.

## Why is it that some paintings are still considered masterpieces even though they don't respect the rules?

During the Renaissance, the painter changes social status—from artisan, he becomes artist. More importance is granted to his personality and his creativity. The artist can afford to be daring in the choice of themes, compositions, or techniques that will make him noticed. People appreciate the originality of the piece, measured by the individuality of his expression. However, this singularity is not enough to distinguish the artist. In order for his work to reach the rank of masterpiece, even though he is straying from the commonly accepted rules, he needs to be recognized by amateurs and a museum's public.

## Masterpieces as training for artists

Observation and analysis of the old masters' works had always been considered an important element in an artist's training. Moreover, the initial purpose of the Louvre was to present the best works of art, in order to train future painters and sculptors in their craft. For them, a masterpiece was a certain idea of perfection, an exemplary work. They were invited to copy these pieces, considered by their instructors as the quintessence of their art.

## Are all the masterpieces in the Louvre reception pieces?

No... The notion of masterpiece exceeds its initial definition. Although the criteria of technical and creative maturity are abiding features in defining a masterpiece, the genesis of this notion, as we know it since the Renaissance, puts into play many other factors—the opinions of critics, art historians and artists, culture, the history of the work, museum displays... Thus, we do not know the exact circumstances under which were created the Venus found in Milo, or the Pietà from Villeneuve-lès-Avignon. Yet, today, both are considered to be two of the Louvre's major works.

## Is a masterpiece always immediately considered as such?

Not necessarily... Some pieces, like the *Venus de Milo* or Georges de La Tour's *Christ in the Carpenter's Shop*, fell into oblivion and indifference before being rediscovered and recognized as masterpieces by archeologists and art historians. Over time, the latter have perceived the works' perfection and originality in comparison to other creations from the same era or the same civilization.

## Who decides that a work of art is a masterpiece?

In a certain way, no one and everyone, for it is not enough to decide that a work of art is a masterpiece to make it so.
The notion of masterpiece varies according to the era during which the work is observed and according to its use. A statue which was originally designed for a pagan temple will not be looked at in the same way by men who no longer revere the depicted divinity. Once an object of cult, appreciated in antiquity for its subject and beauty, the work may have been damaged from carelessness, before being distinguished as a masterpiece at the time of its rediscovery.
It is not certain that men contemplating Georges de La Tour's *Christ in the Carpenter's Shop* in the 17th century would have seen anything other than a religious picture designed to support their faith. Today, exhibited in the museum, it is not only contemplated for its expression of faith, but above all for its own artistic qualities.

### The artist?

Nicolas Poussin was particularly satisfied with his *Judgment of Solomon*.
Even though it was important in his career, the painting has never acquired
the status of masterpiece in the eyes of the general public, who is, even today,
often unaware of its existence.

### Perhaps the critic?

Diderot, writing *Salons*—a series of texts written for the Academy's exhibitions
taking place at the Louvre—highly recommended, in his 1763 chronicle, copying
Chardin's *The Skate*. He considered it a masterpiece even though the painting
belonged to a genre that was judged inferior—the still-life. Painters specializing
in this genre aroused much less admiration, because, at the time, it was considered
easier to paint immobile objects than human figures.

### What about the curator?

The curator is, among other things, in charge of the installation of works
in a museum's galleries. He will distinguish by their display the pieces which are
in his eyes masterpieces. Thus, he will highlight such a piece (Chardin's *The Skate*
for instance) by reserving an entire wall for it alone. The rarity of a work, the place an
artist holds in art history or the museum's collections, technical virtuosity—all these
and more—will be determining criteria for a work to rise to the rank of masterpiece.

## Is display in a museum enough to give a work masterpiece status?

Obviously a work owned by a museum benefits from a certain publicity that
contributes in making it known to the general public—it can be seen by everyone,
it is abundantly reproduced in guides and on posters. This mass circulation adds
to its reputation as a masterpiece.

## Did the *Mona Lisa* become famous because it was stolen?

On the 21st of August 1911, a man of Italian extraction, Vicenzo Peruggia, stole the
*Mona Lisa* to bring it back to his country. He was caught while trying to sell
the painting to a Florentine antique dealer who immediately alerted the Louvre.
This wrongdoing, first reported by the press then immortalized by the motion picture
industry, marks a turning point in the painting's history. Before this theft, it was
essentially admired by a public of knowing amateurs. It subsequently reached
universal fame, confirmed today by the large crowds converging on its exhibition site
everyday. And yet today, few are those who have heard of this now unthinkable theft!

## Did the *Mona Lisa* become famous because the woman portrayed might be... a man?

The androgyny of *Mona Lisa*'s features has fascinated numerous commentators. From the end of the 19th century, writers from Symbolist circles, fascinated by androgyny such as Joséphin Péladan, insisted on this ambivalent characteristic of the *Mona Lisa*.

More recently, researchers have attempted, via computer techniques, to artificially age the face represented on the painting, in order to compare it with a drawing kept in Turin and considered by some historians as a self-portrait of the aged Leonardo da Vinci. According to them, the comparison is sufficiently convincing to infer that the *Mona Lisa* is a self-portrait, hence a man. The many commentaries and interpretations raised by the *Mona Lisa* reveal its complexity, its ambiguity, and therefore the talent of its artist.

Some masterpieces are surrounded by so much mystery and raise so many questions that the explanations supplied by art historians seem quite dull and tedious—especially, in comparison with the storybook interpretations offered by writers who make the works their own. A prime example of this is the amazing worldwide success of Dan Brown's *The Da Vinci Code*. It seems, therefore, that a work's capacity to call on the collective imagination is probably another criterion in the defining of a masterpiece.

## The universality of some masterpieces—a magic trick

Some works, such as Titian's *Concert Champêtre* are, through a kind of magic, immediately considered as indisputable masterpieces. An artist offers an original vision. He knows how to best use the means at his disposal to express this vision and turn his art, painting or sculpture, into a rich, irreplaceable language—a language which is so quickly accessible to the viewer, to the enlightened amateur, that the latter adheres to the message delivered.

For a painter or a sculptor, one can suggest that the masterpiece is the reunion of technical means and intrinsic meaning, be it religious, historical or biographical... As for the journeyman's masterpiece, it corresponds to the achievement of balance between technical mastery and the function of the object created.

The ambiguity of the concept of a masterpiece today is that the rules laid down by the Academy no longer exist. Besides, a masterpiece is not just a simple, one-on-one meeting with an art-lover but also a shared meeting with the public at large.

## Is it possible to not like a masterpiece?

Of course! A masterpiece is not necessarily attractive (which is often the case with works from the 20$^{th}$ century); it isn't necessarily touching. It can appeal as much to culture as to personal sensitivity. To look at a work made famous by its quality is one thing, to appreciate it is another.
Though not necessarily easy to manage in the Louvre, a certain intimacy obviously favors their contemplation, hence their appreciation. If art-world professionals are lucky enough to be able to enjoy this face-to-face encounter with the work, it is a much more arduous task for the general public, but, when it happens, the encounter is even more exciting.

## Should you prepare yourself for the contemplation of a masterpiece?

Yes... If you want to understand what makes it exceptional. You shouldn't rely on the magic of a first meeting. Finding out about the work's history, comparing it with other creations from the same era or based on the same subject, are excellent ways of determining why historians or painters have honored it.
To understand a masterpiece, you must of course trust your own feelings.
But heightening them with a curiosity for the history of the work and the place it holds in the artist's career or in the history of art, will be beneficial. This is how Paolo Uccello's *Battle of San Romano*, less than attractive—owing to its poor state of conservation—remains nevertheless a major piece from the Italian Renaissance. Not only is it important because of its size, subject and the multitude of immediately perceptible characters, but also because it is a living legacy of the interest in the expression of perspective and movement as shown by a 15$^{th}$ century Florentine artist.

## Alternative wiewpoints

For each artist, creating a work of art is about making visible—hence sharing— a certain comprehension of the world at a particular time. For each viewer, looking at a work of art is an attempt at finding the path which leads to the artist's vision, at understanding that this vision can cross paths with his own, and, beyond, with that of a much larger community. Indeed, it is because a more or less large community feasts upon a work that it one day reaches the rank of masterpiece.

# What
## is a

**museum?**

What

is a

## museum?

is a

**What**

# museum?

**What**
     is a
         **museum?**

Hubert Robert, *Project for the Disposition of the Grande Galerie*, 1796

## Where does the word *museum* come from?

During antiquity, the term museum—*mouseion* in Greek—referred to sanctuaries dedicated to the muses (goddesses that inspired poets and gave knowledge to men). It also designated places where scholars, philosophers and poets would gather. There, they had at their disposal scientific collections (botany, astronomy, zoology) used to support their studies. Today, the word *museum* is a term that embraces varied types of collections: scientific as well as ethnographic or artistic.

## Where could you see works of art before the creation of our museums?

During antiquity, art depositories were set up in temples that were called *treasuries* or *treasure-houses*. They were made up of donated objects from states, cities or individuals. Among other things, they held ex-votos—often luxurious objects— intended to thank the gods for granting a wish. Paintings would also be exhibited in art or picture galleries called *pinacothèques*. The French term *pinacothèque* comes from the original Greek word, *pinakès*, which designated a picture painted on wood. The oldest *pinacothèque* that we know of was located in Athens, on the Acropolis. In the Middle Ages, the treasures kept in religious edifices were composed of reliquaries—receptacles made by silver or goldsmiths—designed to protect a fragment of clothing, bone or strand of hair once belonging to a saint. You can see examples of these at the Louvre, in the Objets d'Art Department; they come from the treasure-house found at the Saint-Denis Abbey. Paintings could also be seen in churches.
In addition, noblemen such as the Duke of Berry, son of King John the Good, gathered private collections in their châteaux.

## How long have museums existed?

Although the concept of a collection intended for study or contemplation has existed since antiquity, the word *museum* has been used since the Renaissance to qualify the place where these collections are assembled. The term museum has therefore lost the exclusive definition of a scholar's meeting place. It is in Florence, Italy, during the 15th century that the term was deliberately used to qualify Lorenzo the Magnificent's book and gem collections. The next step was the creation of the Capitol Museum of Antiquities in Rome, at the end of the 15th century, which was followed by that of the Belvedere at the Vatican. Paintings and sculptures were also exhibited in galleries (such as the Uffizi Gallery in Florence), or in apartments (*Appartement des Bains* or King's private suite in the Château de Fontainebleau), specially designed for this purpose.

## What is a cabinet of wonders?

The appellation *cabinet de merveilles* or *curiosités* (exhibition room or cabinet of wonders or curios) refers to private collections—often heterogeneous—which were opened from time-to-time to visitors who would make the request. Just as the French word *bibliothèque* designates the place as well as the piece of furniture in which the objects are kept, the *cabinet of wonders* was a place where one could find nature's strange marvels called *naturalia* (seashells, a narwhal horn, a mandrake root...), exotic items (Mexican clothing made of ibis feathers, Chinese lacquerware... ), stuffed animals (crocodiles... ), musical instruments, works of art (gems, silver works, engravings...), medals, rare books or scientific instruments (armillary sphere—the planetary system represented by metal circles... ).

## For whom were museums created?

If treasures preserved in temples and later in churches were available to all, notably pilgrims and religious people, the Renaissance collections were assembled by personalities (kings, princes... ) or art lovers for their own use, hence intended for a happy few belonging to the same social background. Also, artists circulating in the noblemen's sphere had access to those private collections. *Access for all* will become the main difference between the private collection and the present-day museum.

## When were museums first opened to the general public?

It is mainly during the 18th century that museums began opening their doors to a larger group of the general public. England can be looked to as a precursor with the opening of the Ashmolean Museum, dedicated to science, in Oxford in 1683. A few years before the French Revolution, in the reign of Louis XVI, satirical tracts (often provocative and controversial) began demanding the opening of the royal collections to the general public. The desire to democratize knowledge, serving the ideology of the Revolution, favored these initiatives.

## What is a museum's purpose?

Returning to its Greek etymology, a museum is originally a place for study and exchange among scholars.
When it opened in 1793, the Muséum Central des Arts, located in the Louvre Palace, was intended to train artists, offering them the opportunity to study and to copy works of art from the past.

While these missions still exist, they have been enriched. The museum, now open to the general public, has become much more democratic. Everyone now has access to the museum for learning, self-cultivation, for discovery of civilizations, techniques or materials. A museum is a place where you can travel through time and space. It's also a place for contemplation and delectation; it carries on the vocation of private collections formerly exhibited in palace galleries. This is why more and more importance is granted to a presentation that best favors this contemplation. A museum is a place where you must learn to stroll, to take your time and not to try and see everything in one trip.

## Why preserve and protect works of art in a museum?

A museum is also a place for the protection and the preservation of the works of art and the objects it houses. Thanks to the museums of natural history, for example, we can still see species that are extinct today.
The visitor must respect rules that favor this protection, for without them, there would probably be no access to these works; hence, the interdiction to touch, which is often considered a constraint by the public.
Some pieces, such as garden sculpture, worn by rough weather and vandalism on their original sites, are therefore sheltered in the museum's interior.

## Where do the museum pieces come from?

The most prestigious collection in the Louvre is the former Royal Collection, nationalized and granted to the museum during the Revolution of 1789. This is why the museum possesses *Mona Lisa*, which, during the 16th century, belonged to Francis I's collection.
Some pieces, such as *The Seated Scribe*, arrived following foreign archeological expeditions in which French scientists participated. Agreements were reached with countries where the diggings took place, permitting the shared distribution of objects unearthed during the missions.
Numerous private collections were also given to the museum throughout the 19th and 20th centuries. Such is the case of the La Caze *Legacy* (a bequeathed collection), which includes among other things, several still-lifes by Chardin. The *cartels*—"small cards" or labels—are like I.D. cards for the pieces. They generally indicate the origin and the name of the collector if such is the case. Without these donations, the Louvre would not be one of the most prestigious museums in the world. Other pieces, such as Jean-Honoré Fragonard's *Portrait of Diderot* have joined the collections of the Louvre as the result of *payments in kind* (a system which allows a collector or an artist's heirs to pay inheritance taxes with works of art, instead of money). Lastly, museums buy pieces in galleries, from antique dealers, artists, or during auctions.

## Is it true that the Louvre possesses works looted during the Revolution?

Legend would have it that the museum possesses many works looted by French armies, aided in this task by connoisseurs, during the Revolution or the Napoleonic Empire. Yet, most of the ones actually looted were returned after the *Cent-Jours* (Hundred-Days, Napoleon's last period of reign) in 1815. Others were kept only with the agreement of the concerned countries. They were generally the objects of negotiated trades. The most famous one is Veronese's *The Wedding Feast at Cana*, looted in 1797 in Venice. It was kept in 1815 in exchange for Charles Lebrun's *Dinner at Simon's*, today housed by the Accademia Galleries in Venice.

## Do the works change attribution after arriving at the museum?

Of course... Works of art are continually studied once they become part of the collections, and their particular attribution can evolve according to the progress made in archeology or art history. For instance, animal studies today attributed to Pieter Boel were considered for a long time to be the work of François Desportes. Inversely, the *Meditating Philosopher*, which had always been displayed in the Louvre's rooms as a Rembrandt, was later rejected from the artist's corpus (the artist's body of work).
Despite the care taken by the curators in verifying the origins of a piece likely to become part of the collections, it can happen that the museum unfortunately acquires a fake. Such was the case with the *Tiara of Saïtapharnes*, sold to the Louvre in 1896 as a Greco-Scythian headpiece and which had actually just been produced by a Russian silversmith... It is now in the reserve collection!

## Is a work better displayed in a museum than in the place it was intended for?

This is a debate that still creates controversy among art lovers. In a museum, it is relatively complex to display works in a context similar to the one for which they were created, the space and lighting being different in the museum. A museum presentation is always a compromise between constraints linked to the preservation, the space available to the museum and the taste of an era. The choice of frames used for paintings is quite revealing of the latter. The excessively large and ornate frames that appear in 19th century exhibits sometimes disappear in modern-day presentations. One can say that the pieces are generally more visible and better protected in a museum rather than in their original location, that often no longer even exists. Also, transferring them to a museum has sometimes been a way of preserving pieces that would have otherwise been destroyed. This is what happened in the case of the architectural elements from the Middle Ages now exhibited in New York's Cloisters Museum.

## Do all museums display works of art the same way?

Museographics, the science of museum organization, vary from one place to another. They can highlight the piece itself, removing it from external context; for instance, Jean Fouquet's self-portrait on enamel, which was originally a simple decorative element from a *diptych*'s (painting in two parts) frame, has been granted an individual display cabinet in the Objets d'Art Department. They can otherwise attempt to evoke the original context of the piece, as in the *period rooms* that recreate an interior (often the trend in American museums).

## Were some pieces created especially for the Louvre?

In a way, yes... Subsequent to the Revolution of 1789, artists found themselves working for a group much different from the aristocratic families, which used to commission them and had now disappeared. At the time, museums recently opened were among the institutions that allowed creators to work on a monumental scale and on ambitious historical topics—something generally not accessible to private collectors, who were more concerned with acquiring medium sized pieces in harmony with their personal interiors. When the museum was not commissioning them, the artists were still aware that it was one of the few venues encouraging the exhibition and the conservation of monumental pieces. Museums offered, sooner or later, an opportunity for acquisition of large-scale pieces that had not been the subject of a commission. Who did Theodore Gericault or Eugene Delacroix contemplate to sell to, when they were painting respectively *The Raft of the Medusa* and *The Death of Sardanapalus*, if not to a museum?

## Did the museum commission pieces from artists?

Yes...  Artists were solicited to decorate the Louvre—Delacroix in the 19th century, to finish the galerie d'Apollon, or Georges Braque in the 20th, for the decoration of the ceiling in the king's anteroom.

## Does the museum still call on contemporary artists today?

Yes... The Louvre does from time-to-time commission them for temporary exhibitions. They are invited to create, taking inspiration from the works displayed in the rooms and they benefit from the opportunity to exhibit in the museum.

## Can all kinds of art be displayed in a museum?

No... The size or the materials used can often be obstacles. Certain installations or performances produced by contemporary artists can no longer be satisfied with the kind of space that a museum or a private collection offers. These are natural or urban landscapes that constitute the material and the exhibition venue at the same time: Christo wrapping the Pont Neuf in Paris, *The Gates* in Central Park in New York; or Ernest Pignon-Ernest creating plant sculptures, which call on the phenomena of photosynthesis, in the Pourtalès Park in Strasbourg.

## Can a museum sell or trade works of art?

Not in France... A French museum that is run by the State or the territorial collectivities, cannot sell off what it holds. This is unlike American museums that sometimes let go of part of their collection to buy other pieces, as the Guggenheim in New York has done.

## Are there only masterpieces in a museum?

No... A masterpiece is the exception, the rare gem in an artist's career. Although a museum will generally display high quality pieces, it is impossible that it would only possess masterpieces.
The Louvre, for instance, has a rather encyclopedic vocation. It presents civilizations and artistic periods in the most complete manner possible, with examples of the most interesting creations to be found. The works are not necessarily masterpieces—some present an artistic interest, some a historical one, others are anecdotal...

## Are the museum pieces in their original state?

This is very rare. They often reach the museum damaged, incomplete, sometimes even altered by other artists over time. Some canvases have been cut or stretched (Caravaggio's *Fortune Teller*). Often, time has altered their colors, a result of the instability of the materials used. For instance, in Gericault's *The Raft of the Medusa* the lead-based siccative—a product that helps the paint dry—has darkened.
On some paintings, details have been altered—this is called a repaint, that is to say a modification which has, over the course of centuries, been undertaken by an artist, often different from the original painter, and which can alter the painting's colors or composition. Curators can decide to remove the repaints during a restoration. Such was the case with Bernard Van Orley's *Holy Family* which had undergone what is known as prudish repainting—Jesus's genitals had been concealed by a draping.

Other statues have been broken, *polyptychs* (paintings in several parts) have been dismembered, pieces of furniture are worn out. The list of misadventures suffered by works of art is long. It is sometimes quite difficult to imagine how a work actually looked when first created.

## Is reworking a piece of art found in a museum permitted?

If certain pieces have undergone numerous transformations in their life previous to entering the museum, once in a public collection, they will no longer be radically altered.

Nevertheless, they will be restored, to preserve them better or to make them easier to view. In this way, for example, a broken antique vase might be completed by use of molded elements, to help the viewer better perceive its shape. On the other hand, it is out of the question to complete a mutilated sculpture today, which was not always the case. We favor the authenticity of preserved fragments to reparations. A painting can also be cleaned when time has darkened its varnish, even though it is always tricky to do any further repairs without creating controversy. Any restoration implies deciding beforehand the state of the work we are looking to present— its original state (most often impossible to determine) or the one altered by the taste of a later era.

At any rate, when you decide to fill in a gap to make the subject more clearly understood, the current rule is that first, the operation should be visibly obvious, so that there can be no confusion with the original parts and second, that it should be reversible. A restoration should not fundamentally alter the condition of a work of art; it must be possible to go back to a previous state, according to the advances in historical research on the piece and technical research in the field of restoration.

## Do museums display originals or copies?

The Originals! It is the real *Mona Lisa*! This justifies the sums spent for their security, and the rules that all visitors must abide by when visiting a museum: do not touch, do not eat, do not drink, avoid flash photography…

The decision to display originals often astonishes some people. However, this is what guarantees the training of the faithful and patient visitor's eye. Looking at a copy is somewhat like listening to a new interpretation of a song's original classic version. It sounds like the original version, but it doesn't sound exactly the same! In order to convince yourself of the difference between an original and a copy, compare the copies of the Louvre sculptures displayed in the Louvre Metro Station with the originals exhibited in the museum. You will notice that the color, volumes and rendering of detail are not exactly the same.

## Is operating a museum expensive?

Yes... The Louvre has a budget of more than 100 million euros per year for maintaining galleries and works, acquiring new pieces, organizing temporary exhibitions, concerts, symposiums, conferences, workshops. There are 1,800 employees from about forty different trades (gilders to electricians as well as curators, lecturers, artists and technical specialists, administrators, security agents and reception crews...). The Louvre is comparable to a real city of which the public only sees a small part.

The museum benefits from corporate sponsorship for particularly expensive specific operations, such as the restoration of the galerie d'Apollon.

## Does a museum like the Louvre show all the works it possesses?

A deep-rooted legend has it that the Louvre holds hidden treasures in its reserves. Since the inauguration of the Pyramid in 1989, the museum has considerably expanded. It now has enough surface area to allow exhibiting the majority of its collections. Today, the most beautiful and most interesting pieces are displayed. The public would probably be disappointed, should they one day have the opportunity to visit these famous reserves.

## What if there were no museums...

To imagine a world without museums is not to imagine a world without art. Indeed, public places exhibiting art abound—squares, gardens, churches... and, today, forests and deserts, where contemporary artists intervene.

But it would be more difficult to understand one's roots. Indeed, without museums, numerous exemples from the past would not have come down to us today, or otherwise could only be seen in private collections, obviously less accessible than a museum.

# The **Louvre**

From château to museum
From royal collections
to national collections
How to find your way around?
How to prepare for the Louvre?
What should you see?

Hubert Robert, *The Laocoon Room in Louvre*, 1806

# From château to museum

## A fantastic time machine

Who hasn't one day dreamt of traveling back in time? With just a little imagination and an open mind, the Louvre allows you to do so, thanks to its collections (some of the pieces are now almost 7000 years old) and the building itself. Strolling through the Louvre, you are confronted with the history of Paris and of France. Concentrating so intently on the museum, we almost forget about the palace itself. So let's put the works of art aside for a moment and take a closer look at the walls. From the semi-obscurity of the medieval Louvre to the illumination of the Pyramid, nine centuries look down upon you! Over the course of these last nine centuries, very few people have had the opportunity to see the building without scaffolding and work in progress. It has been in a state of perpetual construction, constantly altered and extended. The Pyramid is only one of these major transformations.

## A fortified château during the Middle Ages

**Why build a fortified château?** The Louvre was not always situated in the heart of the city as it is today. In the 13th century, its location was actually outside the fortified walls of the city of Paris. It was built under the reign of Philippe Auguste, on the west side of the city's walls, with the aim of better controlling access to the Seine River. Far from being a spacious and comfortable palace, it was essentially a defensive element for the city of Paris. Over the course of time, the city grew, eventually surrounding the château and transforming the fortress into a dwelling place for kings. In the 14th century, Charles V ordered the building of a second exterior wall with the aim of protecting the new districts. It can still be seen under the Arc de Triomphe du Carrousel.

**Today, what remains of the fortified château?** It is difficult today to picture this fortress with its ten towers overlooked by a donjon. Whatever is left remains buried in the museum's underground levels. To discover the ruins of the fortified château, you must access through the Sully entrance and walk downstairs to the strange and disconcerting place that is the Louvre's medieval archeological crypt.

The large corridor, with two stone walls running along its sides, corresponds to the former ditch surrounding the fortress—the moats. Like many other fortified châteaux, the Louvre was protected by a stone ditch, blocked on each side, and filled with water. In other words, in the 13th century, here, you would have been walking in water.

The bulges that appear at regular intervals correspond to the base of the towers. But since we are underground, a mere 25 meters are missing. This is the equivalent of five stories!

When looking intently, here and there, you can see signs—mostly heart-shaped—engraved in the stone. These are stonecutters' marks, their signatures. Thanks to these, the number of stones that had been cut by each artisan could be counted, and, consequently, their pay calculated.

**Destruction.** The first great transformation of the Louvre would have been the demolition of the donjon followed by the towers and walls that took place throughout the 16th and 17th centuries. Once a fortress, the Louvre was to become a palace...

## Court life during the renaissance

**Entertainment—the ballroom.** To attend a ball given by the king, one would first enter the Salle des Cariatides or caryatid room situated on the ground floor (a caryatid is the sculpted form of a woman supporting a cornice). This room was commissioned in the 16th century by King Francis I, and completed under the reign of Henry II. Musicians would set up on, and play from the balcony supported by Jean Goujon's famous caryatids. Try and picture the ballroom filled with lavishly dressed members of the King's Court. Of course, the Greek sculptures displayed here today were not in place, thus leaving the entire space to the dancers.

**Visiting the sovereign—the king's pavilion.** On the first floor are the king's apartments, reached by climbing the Henry II staircase, the oldest one in the Louvre. Even though the steps are worn out, the ceiling has kept its beautiful decoration from the 16th century and you can still see on it the letter H, the monogram of Henry II, the sovereign who ordered the completion of this staircase.

Not just anybody had access to the king's apartments! Convention would have it that one cross the guards' room and show their credentials. Now housing the Greek bronze collection, this room has not kept its original appearance. Afterwards, one would reach the anteroom and wait for His Majesty's decision, in the company of courtesans also authorized to see the king. The sculpted wood ceiling, only remaining vestige of the king's apartment, presents today a curious mix of artistic styles from the 16th and 20th centuries, with amusing blue birds by Georges Braque that were commissioned.

You now find yourself in the King's Pavilion, first stage in the construction of the palace that would need four centuries to be completed. It had only taken ten years to construct the fortress, which was much more modest in size.

## A fire during the reign of Louis XIV

**The Petite Galerie (Small Gallery) disappears.** On 6th February 1661, a ballet was to be given in the Petite Galerie (Small Gallery), next to the king's apartments. The decorators were busy preparing the show when all of a sudden... Fire! Fire! The Petite Galerie was burning, and with it, all the portraits of kings and queens commissioned by Henry IV.

**The Galerie d'Apollon is created.** Louis XIV decided to have the gallery rebuilt, as it was initially the connection to the high wall protecting the château along the Seine. With the help of Le Vau and Lebrun, the architect and the painter who would later contribute to the palace in Versailles, the king created the new Galerie d'Apollon, a place dedicated to Apollo, god of sun and the arts—a tribute to the god of sun made by the Sun King (le Roi Soleil), Louis XIV himself.

On the gallery's ceilings, the different hours of the day, the signs of the zodiac, the months evoked through pictures of workers in the field, culminate in the center with an image of Apollo fighting a python—illumination versus obscurity.

**Abandon.** The Galerie d'Apollon most likely inspired the Galerie des Glaces (Hall of Mirrors) in the Château de Versailles; the two galleries look quite similar. The painter, Lebrun, happens to be at the origin of both.

Louis XIV abandoned the Louvre, making Versailles his favored place of residence and the seat of his government. Thus the artists were able to move in little by little.

## Such a long gallery

**A passageway to the Tuileries.** To take a trip to the country in the 17th century, no need to leave the palace. All you had to do was go through the appropriately named Grande Galerie (Great Gallery) that was nearly five hundred meters long. Also referred to as the "Galerie au Bord de l'Eau" (gallery on the waterfront) because it stretches along the Seine River, King Henry IV commissioned it to have easier access to the Palais des Tuileries. No longer in existence, this palace was situated outside the ramparts. These walls had been built under the reign of Charles V at the other end of the Tuileries Garden, which was then located outside the city walls. Thus, the gallery allowed you to leave Paris without being seen.

**Artists' studios in the Louvre.** Since the reign of Henry IV, artists and artisans working for the king had studios at their disposition in the Louvre, underneath the Grande Galerie. In the 18th century, the palace was overrun by painters and sculptors. Some of the works exhibited in the museum were actually created in the palace's studios and workshops.

## A palace for the arts during the Age of Enlightenment

**Artist studios, Academy and Salon.** Picture the palace buzzing with people—painters and sculptors calling out to each other from one studio or apartment to another. In the 18th century, the Louvre was almost entirely devoted to the arts; the Academy of Painting and Sculpture held its meetings here. But the big event was the academicians' painting and sculpture exhibition—its members being the only ones allowed to present their works. The exhibition took place in one of the palace's rooms called the Salon Carré—literally the "square shaped sitting room." Soon enough, people began saying that they were going to "the Salon" instead of to "the exhibition." The term stuck and is still used in French today as the term for an art show.

**The museum.** Numerous were those who requested the presentation of the works in the Royal Collection for the general public. A museum was finally opened for this purpose in 1793. What better place to house it than the Louvre, palace abandoned by kings and invaded by artists?

Alas, the palace was in poor condition. Not only did it need to be restored, it also required adaptation for housing the permanent exhibition of works for public viewing. An example, among many others, of the compromise between the history of the palace and its new vocation as a museum is found in the former apartments of Anne d'Autriche—painted ceilings from the 17th century (by Italian artist Romanelli) and red marble walls which were set up in the 19th century to recall Roman temples. Today these rooms are dedicated to Roman art.

## The end of reconstruction

**The construction of the Ministry.** It is Napoleon III who gave the Louvre its definitive structure. He ordered the building of a wing attached to the Grande Galerie. This new building, now known as the Aile Richelieu (Richelieu Wing), was later assigned to the Ministry of Finance. Civil servants bustled about in numerous offices, in stark contrast with the ceremonial apartments of the Duke de Morny, which can still be seen today.

**The expansion of the museum.** As the museum's collection grew, the Louvre finally annexed the Ministry of Finance in the 20th century. This was part of the project bearing the evocative name, Grand Louvre (Greater Louvre). The Aile Richelieu, with the Cour Marly and Cour Puget (Marly and Puget Courtyards), constituted a space large enough to accommodate sculptures coming from the royal gardens of Marly and Versailles, among others. Their rooftops, now made of glass, permit passage of the natural light under which these sculptures were first created. These rooms are one of the Grand Louvre's greatest successes and make the building itself foremost among the museum's works of art.

## A pyramid in the Louvre

**A labyrinth.** Today, the museum encompasses almost the entire building. It is so huge that it is almost impossible for the uninformed visitor to cross the museum from one side to the other without getting lost. Le Louvre is indeed one of the largest museums in the world today!

**A central reception area.** Although quite vast, the museum still suffers from a lack of space. This is why reception areas have been centralized beneath the Pyramid. Designed by architect Ieoh Ming Pei, the construction was cause for much discussion and not always of the benevolent kind. Among other comments, it was blamed for defacing the façades of the Louvre and for breaking up the perspective which crosses Paris east to west ending at the Arch at La Défense.

Nevertheless, it is a universally known landmark, which consistently highlights the rather heterogeneous architecture of a building that today enters its ninth century of evolution. Thanks to the Pyramid, there is additional space for presentation of art works in the palace; and what's more, its location, in the center of the Cour Napoléon, allows faster access to each of the museum's wings.

# From royal collections
# to national collections

## From salon to museum

From King Charles V's collection of illuminated (hand-painted) manuscripts to
the 18th century's Salon, the Louvre has always housed and exhibited works of art.
This large space, deserted by the king in the 17th century and left in poor condition,
was saved by the installation of the museum, consisting in part of the royal collections.
Initially planned by the royal administration, the Central Museum of Arts finally opened
on August 10th, 1793—the date commemorating the fall of the royalty. A political,
as well as cultural issue, the Louvre Palace was undertaking a new career.

## A museum of masterpieces—proof of France's influence and power

Visiting the Louvre during the Revolution and the Napoleonic Empire must have been
an extraordinary experience. As the royal collections were not all-encompassing,
the museum director since 1802, Dominique Vivant Denon, followed the French forces
in order to gather new material. Being a museum director in those days was no piece
of cake! The most beautiful works of art would be selected in Italy, Prussia, Belgium,
Spain, before sending them on to Paris. Despite his questionable appropriation
methods, the museum aroused the amazement and admiration of many a traveler.
One of the present wings in the palace bears the name of this outstanding museum
manager, who was forced to return most of these works of art after the Hundred-
Days. What remained afterwards was essentially the former royal collections
now "nationalized."

## A taste for the Orient

Little by little, throughout the 19th century, the museum, which until then had focused
on painting, drawing and Greco-Roman sculpture, began progressively creating new
departments. The Campaign in Egypt triggered a veritable craze for all things Middle
Eastern. This frenzy could be felt through the collections' development during the
19th century—the Louvre houses one of the oldest departments of Egyptian antiques
(second to the Museum of Turin). Created in 1826, it was initially directed by
Champollion. And it was followed in the middle of the 19th century by the opening of
the Department of Oriental Antiquities with its famous Assyrian Bulls—shipped to
Paris after excavations undertaken by Paul-Emile Botta.

## An encyclopedic vocation

Even though displaying a wide range of works from many different civilizations, the museum's collections are not exhaustive; for instance, you won't find Asian art works here.

The museum was initially managed by painters and art amateurs. It progressively evolved towards a more objective enrichment of its collections. Art history and archeology gradually became fields of scientific study, entailing a professionalization of the related posts—for instance the creation of the curator's position, which used to be held by enlightened art amateurs.

In each field, the collections are composed with the desire to show the most complete and representative panorama of cultures and movements that are presented there. Even though the collections are mostly made up of masterpieces, this is not the only criterion involved in their evolution. For instance, the museum will look to acquire pieces from an era or an artist that is hardly, if at all, represented. Notwithstanding the quality of the piece, it is impossible to constantly acquire masterpieces, which are becoming much more rare in today's art market. However, this does still happen, as attests the recent acquisition of Antonello da Messina's *Christ at the Column*.

# How to find your way around?

So large is the museum and so diversified and abundant are its collections
that visiting the Louvre can seem like an obstacle course. Here are a few tips to help
you better understand the way it is organized.

## Setting up a museum in a palace is not an easy thing to do

You should keep in mind that the museum is above all an historic building and
a former royal palace, even though it has been largely transformed and refurbished.
Preserving traces of the museum's past is an obligation. However, this constraint
hinders the perfect adaptation of the rooms for the presentation of art works.
For instance, it is obligatory to preserve the existing traces of the royal apartments'
decoration. This is why you will see Egyptian pieces sharing a room with ceilings
from the 17th century. Turning the Grande Galerie into a series of small rooms,
each dedicated to a particular era or a particular artist, would indeed be much
more comfortable; but this would erase traces of the building's historical past.
Incorporating the museum into the palace involves a necessary compromise
between retaining the site's historical elements and the constraints of exhibition
imposed by the art works. Nevertheless, it also happens that historical coincidences
favor encounters. Thus, the Greek sculpture installation in the Renaissance decor
of the Caryatid Room, influenced by antiquity, seems like a match made in heaven.

## Painting upstairs, sculpture downstairs

Often, in the maze of the Louvre, mere common sense can help you find your way.
Since no wooden floor could withstand their weight, the large-scale sculptures
made of marble or bronze are displayed on the ground floor. No need then to look
for them upstairs. The only exception is the *Victoire de Samothrace* (Winged Victory
of Samothrace) which besides its weight issue also raised size problems.
The Victoire's staircase was for a long time the only place strong and tall enough
to accommodate it.
As for paintings, they are systematically displayed on the upper floor, in order to
benefit from overhead natural lighting. This also avoids reflections produced by light
being cast from lateral windows. For this purpose, all the rooftops have been fitted
with glass that let natural light filter in. Where there is an intermediary floor,
you will find small-scale sculptures, ceramics and art objects.

## A place for each piece and each piece in its place

Order governs abundance: the works of art are grouped by civilization, school, country, region and century. Presentation generally follows a chronological order with the exception of some departments, such as the Egyptian section, which also offers a thematic visit highly appropriate to the richness of its collection.
Sometimes, a work's size leads to bending the rules of rational arrangement. Thus, French paintings from the 19th century are distributed according to their size, in two spots quite distant from one another.
Also, in order to respect a donor's wish, some private collections are displayed as a whole, outside the usual chronological routes. They let you perceive the history of the taste of a particular era or individual; their presentation separately is thus very instructive.

## Caution: fragile works

Another determining factor in the presentation of the works are the constraints of conservation implying certain exceptions to the chronological approach. For instance, works on paper, particularly sensitive to light, are presented apart in dimly lit rooms. In order to avoid theft, small objects, including paintings, are placed in display cabinets. You shouldn't be surprised then to find works by the same artist in two different rooms, each fitted to the objects' specific nature.

## Are all the pieces on permanent display?

No. Drawings, because of their fragility and sensitivity to light, are only displayed in rotation on the occasion of thematic exhibitions.
Some pieces momentarily disappear, loaned to other institutions for temporary exhibitions or for restoration purposes.
The Louvre also offers the opportunity to visit temporary exhibitions located underneath the Pyramid or spread out in the museum's different rooms.
These exhibitions are often made up of works coming from the Louvre itself, from other museums or private collections.

# How to prepare for the Louvre?

## Motivate your children

If opportunity permits, when taking the Métro Line N°1 with your children, step out at the Louvre-Rivoli station where they can see copies of some of the Louvre's sculptures. Tell them where the originals can be seen. Take them to the Jardin des Tuileries (Tuileries Garden) and show them some of the statues that can also be seen in the Cour Marly (Marly Courtyard). End your walk by taking a look at the Pyramid from outside. Stop in the Passage Richelieu from where you will have a good view onto the sculpture rooms' interiors. Access to the Passage Richelieu is free.

## How much does it cost?

There is no admission charge for those under eighteen (bring an I.D. card). On Friday evenings, those under twenty-six enter for free, and others benefit from a reduced rate. So take advantage of it; no movie theater offers this! There are several subscription cards offering unlimited access to other categories of the public, permitting unlimited entry for a few days to an entire year (see the Useful Tips section for a summary). If you find the subscriptions expensive, please keep in mind that in a museum like the Louvre, they will help you save time, annoyance, and ensure that you enjoy the museum in complete serenity, which is, of course, priceless!

## Ask for a map on your arrival

Upon arrival at the museum, ask for maps at the circular Welcome Desk beneath the Pyramid. They will come in handy when you start trying to locate the museum's major works, as well as restrooms and cafeterias. Take advantage of your stop to ask which galleries are open or closed.

## Are there documents or free services to help prepare a visit?

Yes... In the rooms where works are displayed, information cards about an era, a material or a style, are at your disposal. Be careful though, these are intended for the informed visitor. It is therefore not a good idea to hand them over directly to children. On the other hand, they will be helpful in completing your knowledge and answering some of your questions.

Certain Friday evenings, in addition to the free or reduced rate admissions, archeology and art history students from L'Ecole du Louvre (The Louvre School of Art) comment on works in all the different sections and answer visitors' questions. It may take a little organization to attend these tours, but it is a good way to hear about art and, above all, to have a chance to freely ask questions.

## Think about the services, intended for children, organized by the museum

Everyday, guided tours and workshops are organized. There is a fee; the various events are presented by lecturers or artists. It's a great way to sensitize your children if you don't yet feel ready to answer their questions. Don't forget that kids enter the museum for free; this way you only have to pay for their guided tour or workshop. While they are being occupied, take time to familiarize yourself with the place for your next visit. Follow one of the presentations destined for adults or, why not ask if you can discreetly listen in on your children's tour.

## Be aware of the distances to be covered

It is preferable to calculate the distance to be covered from the Pyramid in order to avoid a marathon type of visit that exhausts both body and mind. A visit to the Louvre requires a certain physical resistance; for instance, you will sometimes have to cover 200 to 300 meters of galleries intercut with stairs, to reach a work of art such as *Le Scribe Accroupi* (*Seated Scribe*). Be aware that you will have to return the same way in order to exit.

## Chose to see pieces exhibited in the same area

As a matter of fact, it is difficult to see in the same visit, for instance, *Mona Lisa* and the paintings in the Galerie Médicis, which are presented in two opposite wings of the museum. Having to cross several departments to reach the coveted piece can become a real headache. (Because of a lack of personnel, some rooms are closed in rotation every day). Long detours to pass from one section to another are most likely to happen. Moving about with a child in a museum crowd generates fatigue that needs to be considered beforehand.

## Be on the lookout for restrooms

Make sure you take precaution by using the restrooms located beneath the Pyramid. Be aware that the ones situated in the middle of the museum are difficult to find and you may have to stand in line for a while.

# What should you see?

## What can one do in the Louvre?

You can tranquilly stroll about the galleries, draw, attend lectures or workshops, listen to a concert or watch movies in the auditorium, even attend dance recitals.

From a place of preservation and study, the Louvre has gradually turned into a cultural magnet where multiple forms of creativity—past and present—are drawn together.

## What time periods are covered by the Louvre's works of art?

As of 2005, the museum houses nine departments, covering about 7000 years of creation (Oriental Antiquities, Egyptian Antiquities, Greek, Etruscan and Roman Antiquities, Objects d'Art, Graphic Arts, Painting, Sculpture, Islamic Art, African and Oceanic Arts). It treats a period stretching from prehistoric times—with the exception of French prehistory displayed in the Saint-Germain-en-Laye museum—and ending in 1848; to see works created after this date, the visitor must turn to the Orsay Museum.

## Is it possible to see it all in one day?

It's seemingly ambitious to want to see everything in one day. Would you consider reading Tolstoy's *War and Peace* in one day? A visit to the Louvre mustn't be undertaken as an exhaustive study but for the pleasure of pure enjoyment. You will have made the best use of your ticket if you leave serene and enthusiastic, not if you are exhausted and bothered.

## How long can you stay in the museum accompanied by children?

It depends on their age and curiosity level—the younger ones will find it hard to put up with more than a half-hour visit; older ones might think that an hour is too short.

## Target your visit

Keep in mind that the museum receives sixteen to eighteen thousand visitors per day, crowding into 60 000 square feet of space open to visit. It is wiser to choose three to four galleries, in order to avoid fatigue and, all the more, not tire the children, especially the younger ones, who are not used to finding themselves in such large and crowded spaces.

## Are all the museum's departments accessible to children?

All the sections can be visited. Thus, you can choose to visit departments that might appear less than accessible at first glance. You will see such spectacular things as the *Taureaux de Khorsabad* (*Winged Assyrian Bulls*) and the capital from the Apadana Palace in Susa, in the Department of Oriental Antiquities. The gigantic scale of some pieces might be a good way to draw their attention to a world they are not yet familiar with.

## Use what they already know

Start by showing them a piece they have seen in a book or on the web. Play a game of comparisons—size, colors, textures.... Think about the subjects they are studying in class (Egypt, Greece, a king's representation...). Find pieces corresponding to their tastes and interests—a chess player will be delighted with *L'Échiquier de Saint Louis* (*St.Louis's Chessboard*), while representations of mythology's monsters (Perseus freeing Andromeda, Saint George fighting the dragon...) will fascinate fans of dinosaurs and other curious beasts. Mythology, so close to fairy tales, is a good way to help children stop and appreciate a work of art.

## Make sure that the piece you chose can be seen by a child correctly

The display cases have rather high pedestals, making viewing difficult when you're just over three feet tall. The paintings are hung at an adult's eye level. Do not hesitate to crouch and see the works from your child's point of view. You might be surprised to see how reflections can blur the pictures; you may even notice unsuspected details, particularly on large-scale pieces. If you can, pick up your children; for example, lifting them to see inside the *Baptistère de Saint Louis* (*Saint Louis's Baptistry*).

## Are there places to avoid?

Avoid the packed rooms of the Aile Denon (Denon Wing). Because of their size, children will have a hard time here and they will rarely have the opportunity to see the works hidden by adult crowds. Visit preferably the Aile Richelieu (Richelieu Wing), much quieter and whose architecture and works, albeit less famous, are nevertheless breathtaking. Take a trip through the sculpture courtyards (Cour Marly and Cour Puget), the Duke of Morny's apartments, Pierre-Paul Rubens's stunning Galerie Medicis (Medicis Gallery), or visit the *Taureaux de Khorsabad* (*Bulls from Khorsabad*).

## When is the best time for a visit?

To see the most coveted rooms such as the one with *Mona Lisa* or the Egyptian Antiques Department, the low season, just after the Christmas holidays, is preferable. Avoid Easter season, which is the busiest period. If you can't chose the period, be aware that right after opening or just before closing are often the best times for a visit. With older children, you can try and go on a Wednesday or Friday evening when the Louvre closes at 10:00 pm. Part of the museum generally empties around 5:00 pm. This is a quiet moment, favoring observation.

## And then?

It's up to you! During the high season, ice cream trucks and playgrounds in the Jardin des Tuileries (Tuileries Garden) are open and waiting for a well-deserved relaxing moment. A funfair that takes place there at Christmastime and during the summer allows each and everyone to let loose after the concentration required by your visit to the Louvre.

 **1** (page 44)

 **2** (page 48)

 **3** (page 52)

 **7** (page 68)

 **8** (page 72)

 **9** (page 76)

 **13** (page 92)

 **15** (page 100)

 **14** (page 96)

 **16** (page 104)

 **17** (page 108)

 **18** (page 112)

 **22** (page 128)

 **24** (page 136)

 **23** (page 132)

 **28** (page 152)

 **30** (page 160)

 **29** (page 156)

**4**

**5**

**6**

**11**

**10**

**12**

# Reference sheets to the **works** of **art**

**19**

**20**

**21**

**25**

**27**

**26**

**31**

**Are all the departments represented in the references sheets?**
Yes, with the exception of that of Primitive Art, which embraces several pieces from Africa, Oceania and Latin America. Masks, totems, bronze, wood or ceramic sculpture are mainly a prefiguration of works that will soon be presented at the Quai Branly Museum and don't necessarily have their place in the Louvre.

**What are the criteria used for selection of the reference pieces?**

Our objective is to give some historical tools as well as a method for deciphering the pieces, all suitable for children. Therefore, besides the major pieces such as the *Venus de Milo*, *Mona Lisa*, or *The Consecration of Emperor Napoleon*, the works have been chosen for their quality—all of them are considered masterpieces for various reasons—as well as for the rich information they generate, be it on the iconography, techniques or organization of the arts at a given time. For example, we chose Dürer's *Self-portrait* over Poussin's or Rembrandt's—less renowned, it offered the possibility of analyzing this theme from a wider perspective. In the same way, we wanted to present various materials (ivory, metal, stone) in order to address their own specific constraints.
Painting was largely favored. On top of the riches the Painting Department has to offer, this medium seems more accessible to children, who see it as a familiar mode of expression and allows them to be more easily initiated to the mysteries of art history.

# How to use reference sheets to the works of art

## In what order are the references presented?

The reference sheets are classified by department (Greek, Etruscan and Roman Antiquities are together, as are all the paintings), then by school (first the Italian School, then the Northern and lastly the French), with each in chronological order (paintings from the Italian Middle-ages come before the Renaissance ones...).

Because of our desire to remain true to the museum's classification system, rather than a simple chronological presentation, the reference sheets follow the same logical classification as the works presented in each of the museum's rooms. Therefore, this book can also be used as a guide while actually visiting the galleries.

## How do you locate the works in the museum?

The wing, the floor and the department displaying the piece are systematically indicated at the beginning of each reference sheet. On each reference sheet, you will find a thumb index in different colors, indicating the museum wing where the work is displayed.

This color code is taken up in the synoptic chronology and location boards, p. 170, 171.

| Denon | Sully | Richelieu |
|-------|-------|-----------|

## How were the reference sheets developed?

The commentaries proposed in the reference sheets are far from exhaustive, for some of the pieces generate numerous interpretations and controversies. It is impossible to cover and to know everything about these works of art, which is of course part of their richness. The objective here is to propose several different viewpoints as well as information allowing you to prepare answers for the questions that seemed the most obvious to us. To observe a work of art is to wonder about its history and its conception. You can always say that you don't know, stress that the child's question is appropriate, and say that you will look for answers once back home. But, by simply using common sense, you can often furnish plausible elements of answer.

We decided for a method of description and explanation of a work instead of comprehensive categorization of information. This is why the stars next to each paragraph will help you recognize the notions that are intended for the youngest (4-8): ( ✶ ), for the pre-teens (9-12): ( ✶ ) or for teenagers (13-18): ( ✶ ).

It is up to you to use what seems the most appropriate for your children.

## *The Seated Scribe*

2600-2350 BC, painted limestone, eyes inlaid with rock crystal, 53 x 44 cm
Anonymous
Location: Sully, 1st Floor, Egyptian Antiquities

* **He's really scantily clad...**
True, he's only wearing a loincloth, a sort of skirt that men used to wear in ancient Egypt. Because of the heat, longer garments weren't necessary. According to the different eras, the lengths of loincloths varied; they were sometimes even pleated.

* **Yet he's wearing a hat!**
No, he's not wearing a hat but his close-cropped hair. The artist simply stylized the hair's roots. Sometimes, the Egyptians also wore wigs, which made their hair look much longer.

* **What has he got spread out across his knees?**
A papyrus scroll. It was used for writing, kind of like our paper. It was made out of a plant called papyrus. These plants grew along the Nile, the great river crossing Egypt from south to north. In those days, people didn't write in a notebook made of a ream of bound paper, but on a single long sheet that you would unroll like this.

* **He seems to be holding something in his right hand.**
He was probably holding a *calamus*, which has since disappeared. The calamus (a Latin word) was the writing tool of the day, like a pen, only cut from a reed. You can still see the hole where it was fixed in the statue's hand.

* **What is a scribe?**
Scribes were men who could read and write. They were traditionally represented sitting cross-legged, and not "crouching" as he'd been so called. Auguste Mariette, the archeologist who in 1850 discovered this sculpture in a tomb, is responsible for the erroneous appellation "Crouching Scribe," since he described it then as "a scribe crouching in oriental fashion" (*un scribe accroupi à l'oriental*).

* **Why would you want to have your picture made while you are writing?**
In ancient Egypt, writing and reading were a privilege. Going to school to learn to read and write is taken for granted today; one almost forgets that, hardly more than a century ago, there were numerous illiterate people. Such was the case in ancient Egypt, where only princes and members of the administration could learn one of the sciences allowing them to occupy the highest positions in Pharaonic Egypt. Our character was thus a very important man, and probably an influential one too, despite the simplicity of his appearance.

**45**

**✳ Do we know the scribe's name?**

Unfortunately not. Generally, the name of the character portrayed is inscribed on the statue's base. Alas, this one hasn't been found. He could have been a prince, a writer or a civil servant. The statue was discovered in a tomb in Saqqara.

**✳ He was a bon-vivant!**

That's right. He's got a few fat rolls. But this was the sign of his important position. A scribe wrote and administrated. His was a sedentary position, unlike soldiers or workers. Picturing a few fat rolls was a way of symbolizing the character's rank in society. Besides, just like his hair, the fat rolls are rather simplified. They seem to serve more as a symbolic than realistic description.

**✳ He looks concentrated and attentive.**

This is one of the statue's great qualities. The most remarkable elements are his eyes. The sculptor has attempted to make them look real. He used a clever process: a white stone imitates the cornea, while the rock crystal inlay has been cut to represent the pupil. The whole is set in a copper ring imitating the kind of makeup the Egyptians used to protect their eyes.

**✳ Are there many painted statues?**

Yes, in antiquity as in the Middle Ages, statues were painted. Egyptians would represent men with a dark ochre pigment, while women would be painted in yellow. Their actual skin was not this color. It was a code, a convention. Women, busy with domestic tasks, were portrayed with a light complexion; whereas men, who were busy outside of their home, were represented with a darker tone to evoke their sun-tanned skin. These color codes were also used in more recent European paintings, particularly in mythological representations. In the 18th century for instance, François Boucher pictured Venus, goddess of love, with a white complexion in contrast with her husband Vulcan, whose skin was much darker.

### ✳ Why make a statue for a tomb?

In keeping with their religion, the ancient Egyptians envisioned life after death. Therefore they placed in their tombs all the elements necessary for this afterlife, as well as a statue in the image of the deceased person. Offerings were made to the statues, such as food that was cooked for the dead. Thanks to these customs, we have a wealth of information about the culture of these people, despite the fact that they lived more than 4 000 years ago.

## *Winged Assyrian Bulls*

715-707 BC, gypsum, 4.20 x 4.36 m
Anonymous
Location: Richelieu, Mezzanine, Oriental Antiquities

**✳  Do these statues represent men or animals?**
These are mythical creatures with the body of a bull and a human head. Looking from the side, you can see that they even have wings. During antiquity and in   the Middle Ages, creating composite beings was quite frequent—for example, the Egyptians' *sphinx* mixes man and animal (the body of a lion with the head of a man); and the *griffin* mixes different species (a lion with the head of an eagle).

**✳  Their hair and beards are curly.**
As often with sculptures from antiquity, the hair and the beard are represented with curly lines that are not necessarily very realistic. Here, even the bull's coat is represented in this manner.

**✳  Why do they have two pairs of horns?**
The resemblance with actual bull's horns is not intended. They represent a *tiara* (cylindrical headdress) and recall these crea-tures' divine nature. You can find the same symbol on the heads of the winged genies displayed near to the animals.

**✳  Where do these statues come from?**
They were unearthed in the 19th century by French archeologist Paul-Emile Botta in the village of Khorsabad, located near Mossul, Iraq. This village was located on the former site of a gigantic palace with two hundred courtyards and rooms, built by Sargon II at the end of the 8th century BC. Sargon was one of sovereigns of the Assyrian empire that had dominated a good part of the Middle East between the 9th and 7th centuries BC. The arrival of the statues at the Louvre in 1847 marked the opening of the new Oriental Antiquities Department.

**✳ What was their purpose at the palace?**

The bulls were situated on each side of the palace gates. They most likely supported an archway covering the passageway into the palace. In spite of their slightly monstrous appearance, the bulls have a benevolent character and were considered the palace's guardians—protecting it against evil and guaranteeing the stability and security of the building.

Indeed, inscriptions can be seen on their flanks, between the bulls' hooves, containing curses against anyone who would attempt to attack King Sargon's achievements. These inscriptions are made in *cuneiform* (wedge-shaped) writing, which is very different from our occidental alphabet. This style of writing can be found on clay tablets, which, in those days, were used instead of paper.

**✳ They have five hooves.**

It may seem a bit strange, but the design of these statues was meant to be seen from two different points of view—front and profile. From the front, the creatures seem to be stationary, while in profile they seem to move forward. For this purpose, a third leg was added on the side to simulate walking.

**✳ Were there other types of decoration in the palace?**

Yes, the palace was designed as a place for political propaganda and the decoration contributed to the illustration of the sovereign's power. The lower part of the walls was decorated with bas-reliefs—slightly protruding sculptures placed directly on the wall. These bas-reliefs represented scenes of court life (e.g. the king receiving tributes from the Medes, a people under his domination), or protective genies, or the transportation of cedar intended for the palace's rooftops and ornaments. In addition to their decorative purpose, these stone foundations reinforced the stability and resistance of the walls whose upper sections were made of raw brick, a particularly fragile material.

**✳ Why wasn't anybody interested in this palace before the 19th century?**

Because beforehand it had never been localized. It was the people living in Khorsabad who informed Botta of the presence of antique objects. The palace had completely disappeared. Although gigantic, the materials used in the building's construction, such as raw soil, were particularly fragile and could not resist fire or time. The most durable parts, made of stone, were, over time, buried under debris. Excavation was necessary in order to reveal them to the light of day.

**✳ Where do the blocks of stone come from?**
The blocks come from quarries situated above the Tigris. Because
of their size and weight, the obstacles faced in transporting them
to the Khorsabad site were numerous. This is related in documents dating from the time of the palace's construction. They
mention the difficulties in finding necessary manpower to drag the
blocks as well as the problems met when crossing rivers.
As technical means had not greatly evolved in the 19th century,
archeologists did not have an easy time either. Victor Place, Botta's
successor, had to split some of the bulls into pieces in order to
ship them by sea. Unfortunately, Bedouins attacked the convoy;
the statues sunk and never reached Paris.

## *The Winged Victory of Samothrace*

Around 190 BC, Statue in Paros marble, Vessel in grey Lartos marble, h: 3.28 m
Anonymous
Location: Denon, 1ˢᵗ Floor, Greek, Etruscan and Roman Antiquities, Daru Staircase.

3

**★ She looks like an angel.**
That's a fact; the wings bring to mind pictures of angels. In reality, she is the goddess, Victory, who was symbolized by the Greeks of antiquity as a winged woman heralding the positive outcome of a battle. She is also called Nikê, her Greek name. It is not by chance that the famous sports brand Nike should have chosen this name—for centuries now, the name Nikê has evoked a victorious result.

**★ She's flying!**
So it seems. The huge sculpture alone—without the boat serving as base—is more than 10 feet tall and weighs a few tons. Yet, her wings, spread out backwards, give an impression of lightness. The wind makes her garment cling to her body and the long pleats falling diagonally between her legs flow gracefully with the backward movement of the statue's left leg.

**★ She's wearing a see-through dress.**
It's known as a *chiton*. This is the term used to describe the rather long, pleated linen tunic easily recognizable on Greek statues.
The *chiton* allowed the sculptor to show off all the body's details. You can even see her navel. The cloth is clinging as if water had caused it to cling to the skin. Indeed, some historians describe the garment as "wet drapery."

**★ She hasn't got a head!**
Well, she used to have a head of course! As well as two arms which were broken too. By looking at the neck and the shoulders, you can distinctly see where they used to be located. Her wings are justified by the fact that she is a divinity. One of her hands was found in the same location as the rest of the sculpture. This fragment is exposed in a display cabinet next to the statue. Comparing your hand with the statue's hand helps you realize just how huge she is.

**★ What was she doing with her arms?**
It is believed that the goddess was raising her right arm in victory; there is no information available concerning the second arm. Other known representations of the goddess Victory show her blowing a horn to herald good news. The Victory theme can frequently be seen, amongst others, in Philippe de Champaigne's portrait of *King Louis XIII Crowned by Victory - After the Siege of La Rochelle.*

### Where was it placed?

It was in a *sanctuary* (a sacred space dedicated to the gods), on top of a hill on the Greek island of Samothrace, which is in the Aegean Sea. Designed to be viewed from afar, the entire movement of her body indicates that one had to place himself on her left side to get the best possible view. Furthermore the right part seems unfinished or less elaborate. At the time, she was encircled by three walls, which made it impossible to walk around her as we do in the museum.

### How was she transported to the museum?

When she was found in 1863, the statue resembled a veritable jigsaw puzzle. She was shattered in more than a hundred pieces. The fragments were shipped to Paris for reconstitution. Behind the wings, you can see the framework, which fix the different pieces together.

### Why make a statue of Victory?

The statue is quite old and it is not easy to reconstruct its entire history. The sanctuary formerly housing it was dedicated to the Cabiri, the divinities protecting sailors. Because of her boat-shaped base, we believe that she was celebrating a naval victory. Archeologists have imagined that the ensemble may have been displayed in a bowl cut into the rock and filled with water, evoking the sea. But it is sometimes rather difficult to try and draw words from the mouth of a mute statue, no matter how famous she is...

### It must be quite difficult to exhibit such a work.

Very heavy and very tall, the Victory poses a great many problems in her exhibition... For a long time it was displayed in the Louvre's ground floor rooms, however, she was deprived of her wings! The ceiling may look high, yet these palace rooms are not high enough to receive an ensemble, which is more than 10 feet tall at its wing tips. She was finally put on display in the staircase that is sufficiently recent and strong enough to support her weight. But she's really the only sculpture of this weight presented on the upper floors.

* **Symbol of the Louvre.**
  She was for a long time one of the first pieces of art you could see
  when entering the museum. Before construction of the Pyramid, the
  staircase where she is displayed today was formerly the museum's
  entrance. For a brief moment, the museum considered placing her
  beneath the Pyramid, where she would have continued her role
  as hostess.

*Aphrodite*, known as *Venus de Milo*

Around 100 BC, marble, h: 2.02 m
Anonymous
Location: Sully, Ground Floor, Greek, Etruscan and Roman Antiquities

**★ She's got a head but no arms!**

As a matter of fact, she did have arms. But just like those of the *Winged Victory of Samothrace*, they were broken. If you take a closer look at her left shoulder, you can still see a rectangular hole, which probably served to hold her arm. In the hole was a *tenon* (a protruding metal piece) that fitted into two pieces of marble in order to form a joint.

**★ How were they broken?**

This we don't know. When the statue was found in 1820, it was already damaged. In spite of a long and difficult search, her arms were never to be found. She is actually a rather old lady—a bit more than 2100 years old today. When we reach this age it won't be just our arms that are missing...

**★ Who is Milo?**

Milo is actually not a man but a place. It is also referred to as Melos—the name of the Greek island where a peasant discovered the statue, close to an ancient theatre.

**★ Why is she undressed?**

She's not a real woman but a goddess and therefore doesn't live exactly as humans do. This said, the ancient Greeks liked to portray their gods as human in appearance. She is called Venus but her correct name is Aphrodite. Venus is the name the Romans gave her—Aphrodite, her Greek name. She is the goddess of love and feminine beauty and is often represented nude. At the time, to celebrate beauty people thought it necessary to portray the beauty of a naked body.

**★ She has got a piece of cloth around her waist as if she were coming out of her bath.**

Incarnating seduction, Venus was very attentive to caring for her body. The possibility exists that the sculptor depicted her bathing. Legend has it that she was born from sea foam, hence from water. This explains why water and bathing themes are often associated with this goddess. But the Greeks also quite enjoyed playing on the contrast between bare skin and pleated draping.

**✳  What are the two holes on her right arm for?**

They were probably intended to hold a jewel or a bracelet. The Greeks created statues made of mixed materials; white marble was the most sought after. They had quarries in their land, making these statues easier to execute. But they fancied completing a sculpture with metal accessories—one would add an ornament to Venus's arm or a helmet to the head of Athena, the goddess of wisdom and war. Sometimes, parts of the statue would be painted. If you look intently at some of the statues in the Louvre, you can still see traces of color known as polychrome.

**✳  Why is she so famous?**

This isn't easy to understand. One of her many attractions is arguably the artist's talent in representing skin. Marble is a hard, cold stone. It is not easy to make it look like skin. The sculptor mastered the rendering of her curvaceous belly, the dimples on her lower back, the depth of her navel and so many details that recall the observation of a real body. The ancient Greeks were captivated by the representation of reality.

**✳  Her face is not that expressive.**

The faces of the Greek divinities follow a specific code—noses are straight and regular; there is no rupture between the forehead and the bridge of the nose; eyebrows are horizontal, faces oval. The faces' impassiveness evokes the stature of divinity. The faces of statues of Greek divinities are all rather similar. They are not actually portraits.

**✳  Is she made of a single block of stone?**

No. A slit can be seen close to the statue's back, slightly beneath the hips—evidence that she is made of two blocks of stone. It could happen that a sculptor, who didn't have a large enough piece at his disposal, would combine several blocks. The blocks are held together with the help of metal joints, as was the case with the statue's left arm.

**Why did they never fix her arms?**
In the past, missing sections of statues were restored; however we avoid doing this today. An incomplete statue is preferable to a badly restored one. In the 18th century, a statue was named Pollux and belonged to Camille Borghese's collection. When sold to the Louvre during the First Empire, a pair of arms had been attached to the statue. They resembled those of a *pugilist* (a type of wrestler), whereas she was later identified as a *discobolus* (disk thrower).
Today if the missing parts do not pose a problem for viewing, then the piece is presented in its incomplete state. It's up to the visitor to imagine its original form.

**What was the purpose of a statue representing Venus?**
Initially, statues of divinities were intended for sanctuaries where they were worshipped. Yet, it is possible that this statue, executed late in the 1st century BC, was purely ornamental. Anyway, it seems that the design was to be observed from various angles; this can be seen by noting the care the sculptor took in perfecting each point of view. By the way, this explains why it is displayed in the middle of a room—unlike other artworks, more frontal in perspective, which are displayed against the walls.

**Why is she no longer in Greece?**
When she was discovered in 1820, Greece was under Ottoman domination. The French, as many other European nations, were fascinated by Greek civilization, considering it the origin of Western culture. The statue was sold to the Marquis de Rivière, then French Ambassador to the Ottoman government. The Marquis later gave it to King Louis XVIII, who in turn donated it to the Louvre. This is how it came to enrich the Greek, Etruscan and Roman Antiquities Department, created in 1800. At the time, this department displayed models of the perfection of Greek art that artists were invited to imitate.

# Virgin and Child from the Sainte Chapelle

1265-1270, elephant ivory, traces of polychrome, 1.24 x 0.41 m
Anonymous
Location: Richelieu, 1st Floor, Objets d'Art

5

**★ The child has got boy-like short hair yet a dress like a girl!**
The boy portrayed here is Jesus, and as a child, he is never represented with pants. It was customary in the past to dress children in
the same way, whatever their sex. His mother, the Virgin Mary, is
wearing a dress and coat, like the elegant ladies of the Middle
Ages. The sculptor has even represented the embroidery decorating the collars, the sleeves, as well as the edges of the two characters' clothes.

**★ Why are there holes in the Virgin's head?**
She wears a veil that was to be held in place by a crown. The crown
has now disappeared, but we know of its existence through the
reading of ancient descriptions. The holes were for holding the
crown onto her head, the top of which is slightly smaller than the
rest of the skull in order to allow better fixation. Various invento-
ries of the Sainte Chapelle Treasury, to which it belonged, mention
that two different crowns were successively completed—the first
one made of gilded silver, the second made of gold and set with
emeralds. Her dress and the child's were also embellished with
brooches, today replaced by red cabochons. This statue was an
extremely precious object, most likely created for a king.

**★ Are the colors the original ones?**
Yes. In the Middle Ages, as during antiquity, statues were painted—
the seams of the clothes were carried out in gold leaf that was fixed
with a type of glue called *mixtion*. If you look intently, you will see that
even the eyes are painted in blue, with a black pupil. The polychrome
of statues, like that of churches in the Middle Ages, was so fragile
that it has often disappeared, giving this piece even more value. You
would be surprised by the intense colors of religious buildings and
sculptures amongst which the people of the Middle Ages lived.
Several other pieces of the French Sculpture Department still have
traces of their original colors, such as the *Virgin in Majesty* from
Forez or the *Carrières-Saint-Denis Altarpiece*.

**✳ The Virgin is holding the Child in a bizarre way.**
She does indeed carry him rather high; Jesus's body is essentially lying on her hand. This is not very realistic, considering the child's size; he's no longer a baby. The sculptor uses this technique to bring the characters' faces closer together and to give the scene an intimate and familiar quality, enhanced by the smiling expression of the lips. This treatment of the Virgin and Child theme contrasts sharply with more ancient representations, which privileged austerity and gravity. There is no obvious suggestion of the drama that will later unfold in the life of this mother and her child.

**✳ What is the Virgin giving Jesus?**
She is handing him an apple, symbol of Paradise's forbidden fruit, a probable reference to Eve's original sin. In spite of divine interdiction, Eve had eaten from the forbidden fruit. The Virgin—considered as the new Eve, and Jesus—the new Adam, will allow the redemption of this first fault, Original Sin. The Passion drama is evoked here discretely, however perceptible to the initiated, thus leaving room for the statue's grace and elegance, characteristics of thirteenth century Gothic works.

**✳ What is the statue made of?**
This is a rare material, as precious as gold—elephant ivory. It used to be shipped from Africa and would reach Paris by the Seine. In the Middle Ages, the capital had become one of the greatest centers for ivory cutting. Wars, transportation problems and the hazards of elephant hunting, all made for irregular shipments. Therefore, in times of shortage, one would use walrus ivory from Scandinavia, as well as wild boar teeth, stag antlers or even horse, oxen and whale bone. The large altarpiece from Poissy, housed in the Louvre, is made up of a multitude of bone plates.

**✳ How can you tell that it is elephant ivory?**
Because the statue is slightly tilted, you can still perceive the curved shape of the elephant's tusk. Only a tusk would be big enough for an object of this scale to be cut from one single block.

**✳ Is ivory still used in making objects?**

The elephant is now a protected species and the trade of ivory is illegal. There are only a few ivory cutters left in the world today but the craft is now essentially about restoring ancient objects. Original creation can only be made from stocks of ivory gathered before the trade ban.

**✳ Is ivory sculpting similar to stone or wood?**

Though the tools (gouges, chisels, rasps) are similar to the ones used for wood or stone, an ivory cutter is forced to adapt to the size and specific shape of the tusk. He cannot carve very tall or very wide sculptures. He must also take particular care in choosing the right part of the tusk for the intended object. The base of the tusk, equipped with a pulpy cavity—like our own human teeth—easily lends itself to the fabrication of *pyxes*, small round containers for Eucharist wafers; whereas the tusk's main section is suitable for creating human-size figures, plates or mirror cases.

**✳ Is ivory easy to cut?**

No... Ivory has an extremely fine grain which gives it a very smooth surface. This makes it a particularly hard material. The luxury and the fineness of the details obtained are thus remarkable—the precision of a face's contours, the furrows, the suppleness of attitudes rendered by the deep and sometimes hollowed pleats of the drapery...

**✳ Where does this piece come from?**

It was once a part of the Sainte Chapelle's treasury. The Sainte Chapelle is a building situated in the heart of the current Palais de Justice (Courthouse) in Paris and is a place you can still visit today. Commissioned by Saint Louis to receive the relics of the Passion (fragments of the crown of thorns, Christ's blood...), the treasury contained precious objects given by sovereigns or princes.

This treasury was scattered during the Revolution. Part of the works in silver were melted down, while other pieces (reliquaries, precious stones, manuscripts) joined the medals exhibition room, the royal library, or the Saint Denis Treasury. Later, they would either be sold—like the Virgin and Child, to be repurchased by the museum only in 1861—or allotted to the Muséum Central des Arts, the future Louvre—like the *Sepulchre Stone Reliquary*.

## *Basin* known as the *Baptistère de Saint Louis*

Late 13th – early 14th century, brass, engraved silver and gold inlays, 23 x 50 cm
Muhammad ibn al-Zayn (Syria or Egypt)
Location: Richelieu, Mezzanine, Arts of Islam

6

✶ **It's hard to make out the images on the bowl.**
As it is often the case with Islamic art objects, the near totality of the surface (inside and out) is covered with decorative elements. In the middle of this profusion, on the outer surface, you can spot men riding horses—in what are known as medallions, and walking characters—in rectangular cartouches. Next to them are numerous smaller animals (antelopes, boars, dromedary...) and if you look a little bit closer, you will find a bunch of mythical animals (sphinx, griffin and unicorn).

✶ **What is this basin made of?**
It is made of brass, which is a copper and zinc alloy. Small strips of gold and silver, inlayed on the brass surface, enhance its colors, giving this simple basin a highly luxurious quality. Muhammad ibn al-Zayn engraved these plaques with a chisel (a metal tool with a fine point that will slightly incise the metal); the goldsmith used this tool to create details (beards, eyes...). A bituminous black paste, that can still be seen in the hollowed spaces, was used to enhance the contrast of the figurative designs.

✶ **What was it for?**
We suppose that it was used for holding water, because of its shape and the aquatic design in the bottom. You can see the inside by using the footstep next to the display case. You will be able to make out eels, jellyfish and crabs arranged in a rosette, creating a dynamic rotating movement. Its use as a water container explains why it was called a *baptistery* in France.
Indeed, the ceremonial purification of baptism is practiced by immersion or the sprinkling of holy water, with the help of a vat called a baptistery; it is the act of entry into the Christian community.

✶ **Was it really used as a baptistery?**
The basin could not have been used for King Saint Louis's baptism, as it was manufactured after his death. But a tradition dating from the 18th century—its origin unknown—attributed this basin to King Saint Louis. Indeed, in the 18th century many works were attributed to Saint Louis, just to qualify them with remote dating of the Middle Ages. However, we are certain that this basin was used for the baptism of the Imperial Prince, son of Napoleon III, in 1856.

**✳ The characters portrayed have odd clothes and hairdos.**

They are wearing ancient clothes, fashionable in the Orient, where the basin was created. In fact, the artist wanted to evoke two distinct geographical origins. One is that of the Mamelukes, a Middle Eastern dynasty, originally made up of slaves converted to Islam and educated to constitute the branch of the state's dignitaries in office at the time. Coming from Central Asia, they are easily recognizable with their trapeze-shaped hats, their trousers and their beards. The other inspiration is the Mongols, a people native of the Far East. They are beardless, wear turbans on their heads and long clothing that resemble dresses.

**✳ What are the horsemen portrayed on the outer surface doing?**

In the medallions, two horsemen recall a hunting scene while the other is holding a curved cane that was used for playing polo. This highly prized equestrian sport from Tibet (polo means *ball* in Tibetan) was considered a good way to develop skill, courage and military aptitude. Each player uses a stick allowing them to hit a ball. They try to strike the ball into goals installed on each end of the polo field.

**✳ Who are the walking men?**

The men standing in the cartouches wear symbols of their position. The master of the wardrobe can be identified by the folded towel on his arm; the cupbearer holds a goblet evoking the service of the wine, which he is responsible for. Hunting masters hold various animals on leash. Hunting was actually practiced with three different species— dog, hawks and cheetahs!

**✳ Are the scenes inside the basin identical to the scenes on the outside?**

Not exactly... The cartouches do not picture walking men but men on horseback fighting wars or hunting. In two medallions, princes are portrayed seated on thrones, carried by great felines sporting a cup and bow, symbols of power. Dignitaries, represented with writing case and sword, are the equivalent to ministers.

The entire decoration of the basin supposedly recalls the Mamelukes' greatest war victories as well as the entertainment (banquet, hunting, games) enjoyed after their military victories.

**❋ Who was this piece created for?**

As there is no precise information about its origins, we do not know the circumstances nor when it was imported to France. The inventory of the Château de Vincennes's Sainte Chapelle, which was established in the 18th century, is the earliest document that mentions it. Considering the richness of its ornamentation, it was most likely created for an important figure of the Mameluke Dynasty. Both the Crusades and commerce favored exchanges between the Western and Islamic world, which in the Middle Ages spread as far as Spain, hence allowing the transmission of objects or books.

**❋ Do we know the name of the craftsman who manufactured the *Basin*?**

The basin is signed six times in Arabic, with the name of Muhammad ibn al-Zayn, which is absolutely exceptional, since an artwork is generally signed once. The main signature, placed on the basin's brim, can be easily spotted; this is not the case of the other five signatures, which are hidden in the motifs picturing a basin (on the outside), goblets and thrones (on the inside). Even though the Louvre possesses another bowl by the same individual, we don't know anything about him, as no records concerning him have yet been found.

**❋ Isn't human representation forbidden in the Muslim world?**

No... Human or animal representations are both present in artworks intended for princes' courts, as is proved by the numerous characters featured on miniatures as well as ivory or metal objects.

Though it is true that Islam still hardly tolerates the representation of the human form and displays *iconophobic* (rejection of images) tendencies, it is actually the religious worship of images and idols that is forbidden (Iconoclasm Sura V, 90). God's transcendency cannot be represented. Thus, the pieces intended for palace ornamentation are not theoretically subject to the restriction. On the other hand, this rule is strictly respected within religious buildings. There, you will mostly find calligraphy and abstract ornamentations—mostly based on *arabesques* (etymologically: motifs of Arab origin), as well as geometrical elements such as the ones on the mosque doors displayed next to the *Basin*.

In a certain way, the Islamic world invented a vocabulary that would later be exploited by artists from the Abstract movement, even though for the latter, the plastic or philosophical issues were no longer solely of religious nature.

## Slaves. *Dying Slave* and *Rebel Slave*

1513-1515, marble. *Dying Slave*, h: 2.28 m – *Rebel Slave*, h: 2.09 m
Michelangelo Buonarroti known as Michelangelo (Caprese, 1475 – Rome 1564)
Location: Denon, Ground Floor, Sculpture (Italy)

**★   The characters are extremely tall.**
Yes... They are more than six and a half feet tall. Even without their pedestal, they would overlook most of the museum's visitors.

**★   The back doesn't look finished.**
Initially, the back was not meant to be seen. Viewers were not meant to walk around it; they were only supposed to see the sculptures from the front. Michelangelo therefore didn't think it necessary to complete the back of the figures in detail.

**★   Some parts look uncomplete.**
This is true... You can even see the traces left by the artist's tools—some left just a clean cut in the stone, others left imprints that look like fork marks. Sometimes the marks crisscross; sometimes they are parallel. It is almost like you are actually watching the sculptor at work. Many people have been struck by the "unfinished" look of some of Michelangelo's works.

**★   There's a monkey at one of the men's feet!**
He is not that easy to spot. The sculptor gave the impression that he's coming out of the block of stone as if by magic. It's as if the monkey was actually inside the stone and the sculptor was only using his tools to help free him from his marble prison.

**★   The two statues are in stark contrast.**
Yes they are... One of the slaves has swollen muscles, which make him look like he is fighting. His body is completely tense. The sculptor didn't hesitate to deform the slave's body in order to better portray the effort he puts forth. The other one has a relaxed attitude. We have the impression that he is letting himself go. He is detached and looks like he is giving in.

**★   What were these sculptures intended for?**
They were originally going to decorate Pope Julius II's tomb, for which the Pope had commissioned Michelangelo. Famous men enjoyed having their tombs made by renowned artists. They probably imagined that they would be less quickly forgotten after their death...

## ✳ So why aren't they on Julius II's tomb?

It took Michelangelo forty years to create this monument, which was altered several times. The first project provided about forty sculptures. The final monument, located in Rome in the church of San Pietro in Carcere, houses only seven of them now. The Slaves preserved in the Louvre were created in the framework of the second project; other slaves accompanying them are today in Florence. As the sculptures had not been accepted for the final monument, Michelangelo had given them to Roberto Strozzi, a friend of his living in France. Strozzi, in turn, gave them to the king and they joined the museum's collection in 1794. It is very rare to find sculptures by Michelangelo outside of Italy; most of them are still in the places for which they had been commissioned.

## ✳ Why didn't Michelangelo simply execute his first project?

After the pope's death, the project was judged too expensive. The marble used for the sculptures was indeed one of the most sought-after, but also most costly. Therefore he was asked to reduce the monument's ambitious scale.

## ✳ Why are they called *Slaves*?

Michelangelo has depicted ties around their torsos. One of the two men has his arms tied up behind his back and we can see a strap that cuts into his flesh, above the neck and around the chest. Although the other one's arms are free, he still has a quite visible strap around his chest too. All this evokes prisoners or chained slaves. These are definitely not free men.

## ✳ Why represent slaves on a tomb?

Pope Julius II was actually the benefactor to many artists to whom he commissioned prestigious projects. He had, for instance, commissioned the same Michelangelo to paint the famous decor of the Sistine Chapel.

Michelangelo might have wanted to express the idea that after Julius II's death, the artists, once deprived of his protection, would lose a certain amount of freedom, since they would no longer benefit from the same creative conditions. For Michelangelo, it was also about a truly ambitious representation of his art as sculptor, delivering the shape of a body from the matter that once entrapped it.

**✸   Wasn't it shocking to portray nudes on a pope's tomb?**
It was considered that a talented artist should know how to represent the human body. Therefore, painters and sculptors would
follow anatomy classes—they were drawing either nude models
posing in the artists' studios, or nude sculptures from antiquity.
Sometimes they would also dissect corpses to better observe a
body's constitution, even though this practice was reproved and
condemned by the Church. Popes were great collectors of Antique
works. Rome was a city rich in vestiges. Archeological excavations
were carried out to find traces of the Roman Empire. The popes
had even opened their collections to the artists so that they could
study prestigious works of art from antiquity. The *Slaves* testify
well to their knowledge in anatomy and ancient sculpture.

**✸   At the end of the day, an artist is not free to do what he wants...**
Michelangelo suffered from the numerous changes he had to bring
to his work. He interrupted it many times to execute other commissions. But an artist was always dependent on his sponsor.
Despite the fact that he was much sought-after and very well
known in his day, Michelangelo could not impose all his ideas. He
was constantly obligated to take into account the opinions of his
client who was paying for the piece. The true talent of such an
artist was to be able to make compromises, notwithstanding the
material constraints lying heavy on him, while preserving the originality and the force of his creations.

## Milo of Croton

1671-1682, Carrara marble, 2.70 x 1.40 m
Pierre Puget (Marseille, 1620 – idem, 1694)
Location: Richelieu, Mezzanine, Sculpture (France), Cour Puget

8

## ✶ He's in pain!
Yes... Milo's face is tense; he's screaming. A lion has its claws stuck in his thigh, and is biting him.

## ✶ Why isn't he running away?
Because he can't. His hand is trapped in a split in a tree trunk.

## ✶ Who was Milo of Croton?
In antiquity, Milo was a very well-known athlete. He won the Olympics several times. He was considered a hero in his birth place, the Italian city of Croton.

## ✶ Milo was in good shape.
The sculptor took great care in representing all the different muscles in Milo's body. He sculpted them tensed, in action, thereby showing that Milo is making an effort to free himself from the tree trunk and to protect himself from the lion's attack.

## ✶ How did he get his hand stuck in the first place?
He had made a bet. Even though he was already old, he claimed that he was still strong enough to split a tree's trunk with the mere strength of his arm. Lumberjacks then placed corners to open a crack that Milo was supposed to widen. But Milo had overesti-mated his own strength and his hand got stuck. After nightfall, a wolf came up and devoured him.

## ✶ But it's not a wolf, it's a lion!
The sculptor chose to show Milo defeated by an animal that was more dignified than a wolf. At the time, the lion was considered a symbol of power.

## ✶ What is the purpose of the bowl on the floor?
It is a bowl that symbolizes Milo of Croton's victories at the Olympic games. In this way, anyone could easily identify the hero and better grasp the sense of the story that was being told.

**✳ The lion is in a funny position!**

Yes... It is actually odd to see a lion standing up on its rear legs twisted in this way. Technically speaking, the animal's purpose is to balance the sculpture. Indeed, it would most likely be destabilized by the weight of the marble, if it were not for the balancing support provided by the lion. The lion, just like the trunk, is actually supporting Milo, a bit like a cane or crutches.

**✳ How do you get a lion to pose?**

Puget probably didn't use a real lion for his model, so he most probably put his imagination to work. In the 17th century, it was not easy to see lions in France since there were very few zoos and artists did not travel as far as Africa.

**✳ Who commissioned this statue?**

The King, Louis XIV commissioned Puget to sculpt a block of marble which was stored in Marseille. He authorized Puget to choose his topic, which, in the 17th century, was very rare. The artist decided to portray strength and power—Milo, defeated by time—the lion.

**✳ Where was the statue displayed?**

In Versailles, in what was called the Place d'Honneur (Place of Honor), at the end of the "green carpet"—that is to say the great lawn located behind the château. Despite its audacious theme, the statue was highly praised which was not necessarily a given, since a king like Louis XIV might not have accepted such a blatant warning about the fleeting characteristics of power.

**✳ Was Puget a famous sculptor?**

Let's say he had the king's trust. The latter had commissioned several statues from him, which are today displayed in the Louvre. Puget also worked on decorating building façades in Toulon and royal sailing vessels.

**✹ How do you craft such a sculpture?**
Generally the first thing you do is to make a lot of sketches. For this
piece, one of them has been preserved and can now be found in the
Rennes Museum. Clay was then used to model the sculpture
before the marble cutting. Clay is less costly and it allows an artist
to put into place the composition. This clay layout was kept damp
and, therefore, could be easily altered—you simply added or
removed as much clay as needed. On the other hand, once the
stone cutting work was begun, the sculptor couldn't go back in
time. He had to be careful not to remove too much material. This
last phase, the most delicate part of the work, could take years.
Great attention was required, and he progressed accordingly, in a
precise established order, to cut and sculpt the different parts. The
most fragile parts were treated last, in order to avoid shattering
from the effect of vibrations during the work in progress.

## Marly Horses

1739-1745, marble, 3.40 x 2.84 m
Guillaume Coustou (Lyon, 1677 – Paris, 1746)
Location: Richelieu, Mezzanine, Sculpture (French section), Cour Marly.

**✳ The horses look angry!**
They rear up and neigh, trying to escape the lads attempting to hold them back. Even their manes are standing straight on their heads.

**✳ Why did Guillaume Coustou portray horses rearing up?**
Sovereigns and important figures were often portrayed riding a horse—an example of this is Bernini's statue of Louis XIV next to the Pyramid. The equestrian portrait was a symbol of social and political power. This said, it was much more original to show men standing on the ground and trying to tame the horses; hence, in this sculpture, man is somehow dominated by these animals. Guillaume Coustou is trying to show the lads' strength as measured against that of the horses. This statue is about man measuring himself against the forces of nature without being sure he will prevail.

**✳ Was it usual to treat this kind of topic?**
No... First of all, it entailed too many technical difficulties that had to be solved. Coustou was probably inspired by a famous classical group kept in Rome, called the *Dioscures* (Castor and Pollux—Jupiter's sons), which also shows men trying to tame rearing horses.
On the other hand, the originality of Coustou's piece also lies in the fact that he didn't chose a historical or mythological pretext but an exotic one instead—the two lads are Indian! Although it is difficult to identify, their nationality is nevertheless strongly suggested by a feather hat laying at the foot of the group on the left. Also, note the presence of the animal skin used as a saddle.

**✳ Why did Coustou place stones beneath the horses' stomachs?**
This is not very realistic, since a horse won't rear up if it is standing on rocks! The stones are nevertheless essential—the major technical difficulty with such sculptures is to balance them. Unless you turn them into poles, the horses rear legs would never be strong enough to support the weight of their bodies and heads. Just like in *Milo of Croton's* case, the stones are used as supports. The grooms' bodies also contribute to supporting the ensemble.

**Did grooms live naked?**

Of course not, and it seems actually odd that they should be naked here. Again, like Puget with his *Milo of Croton*, the sculptor was showing his mastery not only in sculpting animals, but also in human anatomy. The nudes are pretexts for rendering the muscular tension of the bodies in movement. Just like Coustou most likely observed real horses in his Parisian studio—situated near the Equestrian Academy—male models probably posed in his studio to inspire him for his work in creating the grooms.

**Where were these statues destined to be seen?**

These statues were to replace two groups of horsemen, respectively entitled *La Renommée* (*Renown*) and *Mercure Chevauchant Pégase* (*Mercury Astride Pegasus*), sculpted by Antoine Coysevox for the Château de Marly. This royal residence, located about twenty kilometers from Paris, had been built following Louis XIV's orders in 1679. Marly was a place intended for the king's private life; it allowed the sovereign to escape the burden of the rules governing daily life in the Versailles Court.

In 1719, Coysevox's horses were moved to the Tuileries. To replace them, Louis XV, Louis XIV's successor, commissioned two other equestrian ensembles for the park at Marly. There, they decorated a pond that was used as a drinking trough for horses. This explains the choice of the equestrian theme.

The four groups—Coysevox's and Coustou's—have now joined the collections of the Louvre, where they are displayed in the same room.

**Where are the bridles so the men can hold the horses?**

Indeed, over time, these particularly fragile parts have been broken. Despite their dimensions, these sculptures have traveled many times—first moved in 1794 from the gardens at Marly to the entrance of the Champs Elysées in Paris, they were later replaced by copies in 1984, and transferred to the Louvre, in order to protect them from pollution. It is thus easy to compare the originals with the copies. The latter, obtained from a casting of the originals, are slightly bigger. Also, the mix of resin and marble powder poured into the mold was not exactly the same color or the same grain as the original stone.

**✳  What kind of stone did Coustou use?**
The marble came from the very prestigious Carrara quarries in Italy—the most sought after because of its particularly fine grain and milky color. Coustou was too busy to make the trip himself, so he entrusted another sculptor, Michelangelo Slodzt, with the choice of the blocks of stone. Slodzt was in Italy at the time and was informed by emissaries of Coustou's work in progress. Selecting the right piece of marble is a delicate task, especially for such large-scale pieces. Indeed, the least flaw in the stone, for instance a vein of a different color, or a weakness due to a crack, can definitely harm the work's realization. Bringing the blocks from Carrara to Paris was no piece of cake either. On account of the material's weight, transport by waterway was the best suited in those days.

**✳  Did the sculptor work alone on these two statues?**
No... He designed the models, which were used for cutting the marble. In the last stage he was assisted by eight assistant sculptors who helped him create the statues from the blocks of marble. Also, since Coustou fell ill, his assistants had to finish them. A sculptor rarely cuts his own works of art. Because of the sculpture's voluminous size and the numerous details (horse tails, manes, bridles), the cutting work—long and delicate—required technical virtuosity. The work was meticulous and great care was taken so that they would not shatter from the vibrations provoked by the cutting. In order to avoid accidents during transportation, the most fragile parts were not executed in the studio, but once the statues had reached their final destination. It took another four years to see the cutting and the installation of the ensemble carried out.

# Saint Francis of Assisi Receiving the Stigmata

Predella: *Innocent III's Vision; the Pope Approving the Order's Statutes;
Saint Francis Preaching to the Birds*
1295-1300, *tempera* on wood, 3.13 x 1.63 m
Giotto di Bondone (Colle di Vespignano, circa 1265 – Florence, 1337)
Location: Denon, 1st Floor – Painting (Italy) – Salon Carré

**There are several different scenes depicted in this painting.**
At this time, paintings were a bit like picture books. Thanks to
them, illiterate people were able to learn about the lives of important figures. This painting's design is almost like a page from a
comic book. The central part relates the most important episode in
a person's life, in this instance Saint Francis. The lower part is
called a predella—a frieze of images relating moments from the
main character's life. Here, St. Francis is always dressed in brown,
which allowed those viewing the painting to easily identify him on
each small image.

**It's all golden.**
Most of the paintings of this period were painted with gilded back-
grounds, not on canvas but on wooden supports. The use of hemp
or linen canvas became more frequent at the end of the 15th century. Gold, in cigarette-paper thin leaves, was applied to the panel.
This technique not only allowed the evocation of divine supernatural light, but was also a way to show off the wealth of a painting's
commissioner—gold being a luxury material par excellence.

**Hands up!**
Saint Francis, the main character, isn't being threatened. Rather,
he is filled with awe because he is witnessing something extraordinary. He sees Christ, arms outstretched as on the cross and in
the form of a seraph—that is to say an angel with three pairs of
wings. Jesus seems to be flying like a bird.

**Is Saint Francis wearing a dress?**
The long brown clothing worn by monks is called a frock. Instead of
a belt, Saint Francis wears a rope tied with three knots, which symbolize the three vows that monks took—poverty, chastity and obe-
dience. Part of his hair is tonsured—shaved bald—as was and still is
the custom for monks. Saint Francis had renounced a comfortable
and easy life in order to live a modest existence and help the poor.

* **It looks like Saint Francis is handling a kite.**
  The golden streaks, which link Christ's hands, feet and sides to the Saint's, actually do look like a kite's strings. Indeed, as a result of this apparition, Saint Francis was said to have kept scars on the palms of his hands, on his feet and on his torso. These wounds are called the stigmata. In order to represent the stigmata, the painter drew lines that are meant to materialize the transmission of Christ's wounds to St. Francis. They correspond to the nails that were hammered into Christ's hands and feet during the Crucifixion, and to the spear blow to the side that was inflicted on him by a Roman soldier. The moment when Christ's wounds appear on Saint Francis's body is called the stigmatization.

* **Saint Francis is really tall!**
  If he were standing, he would surely be taller than Mount Verna, the mountain pictured in the painting's background. The two chapels, represented on St. Francis's left and right, look like dollhouses. In the first scene of the predella, we even see Saint Francis holding a church as if it were just a model. In fact, St. Francis's image is bigger than the rest of the elements in the painting. The artist did this in order to help the public understand that St. Francis is the hero of the story being told in this painting.

* **Giotto is good at rendering volume and space.**
  Yes... and this is one of the most innovative elements of the time. He painted the *contours* of the saint's garment—the fabric is not the same color when it is placed in shadow or in light. What's more, in the first two scenes of the predella, Giotto constructed the space using *perspective*—which means that he attempted to transcribe the illusion of seeing distant objects as smaller than closer ones. The painting doesn't seem flat but rather resembles a box with figurines displayed inside.

## ✳ Symbolic or realistic?

The painting was first intended for the church of San Francesco in Pisa. It made sense then that it would be mostly symbolic. Thus, on the last scene of the predella, a tree suffices to represent the forest where Saint Francis is said to have talked to the birds. It was not necessary to paint it entirely. People living at the time could understand these symbolized images. This said, Giotto was also interested in reproducing certain aspects of reality. For instance, Saint Francis is frowning—hence expressing an emotion, which was a rare thing at the time. In the works of other masters of Giotto's era, faces are depicted completely stiff and expressionless.

## ✳ A great innovator.

As early as the 16th century, Giotto was considered as the artist of the transition, linking the Middle Ages with its artworks that were essentially symbolic representations, to Renaissance artworks that were more concerned with representing the world—not so much from a divine standpoint but rather from a human, or material, point of view.

# Portrait of Lisa Gheradini,
## known as *Mona Lisa*

1503-1506, oil on wood, 77 x 53 cm
Leonardo di ser Piero da Vinci known as Leonardo da Vinci (Vinci, 1452 – Amboise, 1519)
Location: Denon, 1ST Floor - Painting (Italy)

**✳ The painting has a bizarre coloring.**

This is a rather ancient painting, about five hundred years old. It has darkened and yellowed with time. It is quite probable that the original colors were much brighter. Ancient descriptions of the painting have been found, which describe a slightly less drab tone.

**✳ What is the position that she is taking?**

She is sitting on a balcony, with her left hand leaning on the arm of a chair. Looking closely, you can make out a balustrade behind her that separates her from the wild landscape. She is turned slightly towards us, as if she were looking at us.

**✳ She doesn't have eyebrows!**

This woman lived in the 16th century. In those times, fashionable women would pluck their eyebrows. Despite the sophisticated quality of her garments, made of fine fabrics, she is not wearing any make-up, even though most women of her time and rank were obliged to.

**✳ What is her name?**

Today, she has two names: *Mona Lisa*, the name used in the documents from the 16th century, and *La Gioconda*. It is believed that she was a young woman named Lisa Gherardini. She was married to Francesco del Giocondo, a rich bourgeois from the city of Florence.

**✳ Why is she dressed with dark colors?**

This is the type of garment that was suitable for a married woman. It is rather refined and decorated with pieces of embroidery around the neckline. She is wearing a light veil that holds her wavy hair. Her figure, balanced in the shape of a triangle testifies to the self-control required of a woman of her bourgeois standing. Remember, a portrait was always supposed to give the best possible image of the model.

**✳ She looks like she is mocking.**

Her smile is one of the painting's claims to fame. Leonardo da Vinci advised painting faces by conferring upon them the feeling of life. He used the smile to suggest—beyond her young woman's physical appearance—her life and her thoughts.

**✹ She is smiling, but her lips are barely open.**
The artist succeeded in reproducing the suggestion of a smile, which is not easy. No one can pose with the ghost of a smile on the lips for a very long time. The artist proved his great qualities of observation and the mastery of his craft in order to manage to reproduce this expression.

**✹ Playing with light and shadow.**
When you take a closer look, you realize that there is no clear line rendering the contours of the face and the hands. The lips and eyelids are suggested by gradations of lighter or darker colors, according to their position in relation to the light source. Da Vinci largely used these gradations of light and shade called *sfumato* (blurred) in Italian. They allow him, in particular, to increase the relief and volume of certain parts of the painting, such as the model's cheekbones or her hands. They enhance the impression of reality that the artist was looking to recreate.

**✹ The wild landscape doesn't depict Tuscany.**
You can see a path, a river crossed by a bridge and, in the background, high mountains. It is most likely that the artist didn't reproduce an actual, existing site. He made up an imaginary landscape from the ones he had seen during the course of his many journeys. This strange place enhances the slightly mysterious quality of the young woman's smile. Her smile would probably be more insignificant on a flower background. The landscape raises questions and stimulates the viewer's imagination.

**✹ Did the model like the painting?**
We don't know about that. It seems that Leonardo never delivered the portrait to either Lisa Gherardini or her husband. In 1516, when he arrived in France at the invitation of King Francis I, he was still in possession of the painting. This is arguably more than just a portrait—perhaps even one of the artist's many experiments on the theme of facial expressions and light.

**✳ Did Leonardo da Vinci make a living with his painting?**
Leonardo da Vinci was invited to the Italian princes' courts not just as a painter, but mainly as an engineer. He has left numerous sketches prefiguring flying machines and engines of war among others. Though never manufactured, they are testimonies to his constant research. He was asked to design and execute many different things—a network of canals in the city of Milan, stage machinery to be used for festivities, an equestrian statue... He was a man curious about all the aspects of creation, be it artistic or scientific; he was what is called a humanist.

**✳ How did the painting end up in the Louvre?**
It was thanks to Francis I. The painter died in France in 1519 at the age of 67. He had brought along with him several of his paintings, amongst which was the *Mona Lisa*. From the 16th century, the painting was part of the royal collection and displayed in the Château de Fontainebleau. We do not know how the king acquired it. Did he receive the painting as a gift directly from the artist? Did he buy it...? This royal collection became the core of the museum, which opened in 1793.

# *Concert champêtre* (The Pastoral Concert)

Around 1509, oil on canvas, 1.05 x 1.37 m
Tiziano Vecellio, known as Tiziano or Titian (Pieve di Cadore, 1488/1490 – Venice, 1576)
Location: Denon, 1st Floor - Painting (Italy)

✳ **It's the countryside!**
On the painting's right side, we see a shepherd and sheep; in the center, behind the characters, a farm; in the distance, mountains and what looks like water. The sky drifts to red, which leads us to believe that it is the end of the day.

✳ **What are the characters of the group in the foreground doing?**
A man is playing the lute, an old instrument that looks a bit like a guitar. We see his fingers picking the strings. Leaning over in his direction, another man is listening to him. A woman sitting in front of them holds a flute in her hand, yet she is not playing it. Music was very important in the city of Venice, where this painting originates. This is why the group symbolizing a concert—the painting's theme— is at the center of the composition. Finally, a second woman, standing apart, seems to be pouring water into a stone tank.

✳ **Why is the man dressed in red?**
He wears the dress of Venetian nobility in the 16th century—a very plush smock and two-toned tights instead of pants; the sleeves are very large. Owning a garment made with so much fabric proves how wealthy he is. The quality of his clothing tells us that he is not a shepherd. Another hint of his status is the instrument he is playing, which, at the time, was very fashionable among nobility.

✳ **Why is a nobleman playing music for shepherds?**
The artist probably took inspiration from a poem called Arcadia, by Sannazaro, which was published early in the 16th century. The poem told the story of a young nobleman named Sincero who recounts—to the shepherd Carino—his unfortunate love for a young Neapolitan girl, while accompanying himself with a lyre.
The lyre, a chord instrument, was known as an attribute of the god Apollo and of the poet Orpheus. Although inspired by the poem, the painting does not claim to be the literal illustration of it; Titian thus replaced the lyre by a lute, another chord instrument, making a poet out of his character. Wind instruments were the attributes of Bacchus (god of vine and sensuality) and his entourage.

**✳ One especially notices the women.**
The women are very present in the foreground. Their naked skin creates highlights against the darker background where we see the two men and grass. The artist used gradations of light and shadow to enhance the volumes of their bodies. The women's nudity creates an odd contrast with the clothed men.

**✳ Why are the contours blurred?**
The contours of the women's bodies are not clearly defined. It is as if their bodies were blending with the landscape. In this way, the artist gives the impression that the female characters indeed belong to the same space as nature around them. This was an innovation at that time, for painters usually drew contours with great precision. For a few decades already, Venetian painters, followed by Leonardo da Vinci, had been endeavoring to render lighting that would envelop the characters. And from this standpoint, this painting is considered the most successful of its time.

**✳ Why are the women naked when the men are dressed?**
It's true that the situation is strangely preposterous. In fact, the men represent 16th century characters, rooted in real life, while the women embody timeless characters. Which also explains why the men don't seem to notice them, even though they are naked! If they see them, it is in their imagination. It was probably through a desire to mark the difference between real characters and imaginary characters that the painter has represented men in their clothes and women naked.

**✳ What do the women represent?**
They most likely represent *allegories*—that is to say the visual representation of such diverse themes as art, wisdom, or a country, through the materialization of characteristics and attributes. In this case, the two women would respectively symbolize, on the right, beauty, and on the left, moderation. The visual clue that allows us to identify beauty is the presence of a flute—associated with Bacchus, the Roman god of wine and carnal pleasure. This woman would thus personify an invitation to love, which the noble lute player dreams about. As for the beauty's friend, who is holding a pitcher, her presence would suggest level-headedness or good judgment. The allegory of moderation has traditionally used for its emblem two pitchers, one that contains water and the other wine, that are to be mixed. This allegory is also the basis for the French expression *mettre de l'eau dans son vin* which literally means, "to put water in one's wine," or in other words to use moderation.

**What is the woman pouring water into?**
It is perhaps a sarcophagus, a stone coffin used in Antiquity. As a matter of fact, artifacts from Antiquity were so popular in the 16th century that some people began collecting creations from this era. It is thus not surprising that artists would feature these objects, appreciated by art lovers, in their own works.

**For whom was such a painting created?**
Even though we don't know the name of its first owner, it is likely that this piece would have been executed for a private collector. The fact that the painting isn't very big and that its theme is profane seems to indicate that he who commissioned it was cultured—someone capable of appreciating a rather rare topic as well as a technique that was new at the time. Intended for palaces and wealthy residences as well as places of worship, art was no longer just about illustrating religious topics.

**Has this painting always been famous?**
Yes... To such an extent that it was even owned by the Kings of France and that every once in a while, other painters have copied it. It is so famous that throughout the 19th century, it continued to inspire artists. Later, Edouard Manet reinterpreted the *Concert Champêtre* in a painting causing scandal—the *Déjeuner sur l'Herbe*, now at the Musée d'Orsay.

# The Wedding Feast at Cana

1563, oil on canvas, 6.77 x 9.94 m
Paolo Caliari, known as Veronese (Verona, 1528 – Venice, 1588)
Location: Denon, 1st Floor - Painting (Italy)

13

## ✶ This painting is huge!

Indeed it is! More than 22 feet high and 32 feet wide, it is the biggest painting in the Louvre. It represents a wedding party where there are about a hundred characters. Some of them are eating, others are serving dinner, and musicians are entertaining guests. There are even animals—a great number of dogs, including a very tiny one strolling about on the right side of the table, while a cat sharpens its claws on an amphora in the lower right corner of the picture. On the left, you can also spot a parrot on the shoulder of a dwarf, next to the tall character in green, and oh, let's not forget the monkey.

## ✶ What a strange idea to picture people eating!

As the painting was intended to decorate a monnastery's dining hall, the artist was asked to picture a meal. Thus, when the monks gathered for their meal, they were able to admire the great painting that had been created to adorn the entire width of the hall's background wall.

## ✶ Men are wearing dresses!

The painting was executed for the city of Venice, where at the time, wealthy men wore long and luxuriously adorned costumes. Some of the characters are wearing turbans, as Venice was an international trading crossroads where you could meet lots of foreigners and in particular people from the Orient, now referred to as the Middle East.

## ✶ Some of the characters look less richly dressed.

As a matter of fact, this scene doesn't picture a simple wedding banquet, but a biblical theme. The newlywed couple is therefore not the main topic. This also explains why the richly dressed bride and groom are relegated to the extreme left side of the piece, while in the center, soberly dressed, is Christ with a halo, his mother Mary and his first disciples, whose ambition was to live as simply as Christ lived himself. Jesus had been invited to a wedding banquet in the Near Eastern city of Cana. It is said that during this meal, Christ turned water into wine, thereby accomplishing his first miracle.

* **How do you see that a miracle is taking place?**
Let's take a closer look... You can make out several motifs that convey the idea of drinks on the table—a slave dressed in yellow and identifiable by his bare feet (in the foreground on the right) transfers liquid into an ewer, a pitcher that will be used to serve the guests. You can clearly see that he is pouring wine and not water. Behind him is the cupbearer in charge of serving the wine. According to the bible story, he is convinced that the recipients contain water and is therefore puzzled to see wine flowing from the pitcher.

* **How long does it take to paint such a large canvas?**
It depends on many different factors—the number of commissions the artist has to honor at the same time, his rapidity, the demands of the person commissioning the work... As far as this particular painting is concerned, we are very well informed about the details of its commissioning, since the original contract was conserved. It says that the painter had slightly more than a year, fifteen months exactly, to finish the canvas. This is not a lot of time!

*
**Why did Veronese paint on a canvas and not directly onto the dining hall's wall?**
Venice is a city with foundations built in water. When you paint in *fresco*—that is to say, directly on the wall, as was customary for large-scale pieces—the humidity of the foundations seeps up and very quickly damages the murals. Therefore, as of the 15th century, Venetian painters preferred to use canvas that was hung a few inches away from the wall, in order to better protect them from humidity. This also represented a tremendous advantage for the painter who could then paint in his workshop. Nevertheless, in this particular case, the blank canvas had been fastened to the wall and Veronese executed his work directly in the dining hall and shared the monks' life for a few months.

* **Why place Christ in the center instead of the bride?**
  Notwithstanding the number of protagonists pictured on this painting, the main character is Jesus. He is at the focal point of the
  painting, placing him exactly in front of the dining hall's entrance.
  He was thus the first character that you would see when entering
  the room. The monks were thus confronted by Christ—whose
  teachings they must follow—before being able to contemplate the
  material luxury that they had theoretically renounced. Also, the
  hourglass painted on the musicians' table was a constant reminder
  that material pleasures are fleeting.

* **The painting recalls the Last Supper.**
  This is certainly no coincidence. Representing Christ at the center
  of the table in the scene of the *Wedding Feast at Cana* is unusual.
  In general, he is painted off to one side. Veronese was aware of
  this, and he played with the ambiguity of the representation. If The
  *Wedding Feast at Cana* recounts the first miracle—hence the revelation of Jesus's divine nature—the Last Supper recounts his last
  meal, just before the start of the Passion. In one single stroke, the
  artist has grasped Jesus's entire destiny.

# The Fortune-Teller

1594-1595, oil on canvas, 0.99 x 1.31 m
Michelangelo Merisi also know as Il Caravaggio or Caravaggio (Caravaggio, circa 1571 – Porto Ercole, 1610)
Location: Denon, 1st Floor - Painting (Italy) - Grande Galerie

**✳ Why is the woman holding the man's hand?**
This woman is a fortune-teller. She claims that she can tell the future simply by looking at the palm of your hand. Maybe she is about to announce to the young man that he is going to fall in love or that he will make lots of money gambling.

**✳ How do you recognize that she is a fortune-teller?**
At this time, these women were called "Egyptians;" they were the equivalent of our "gypsies" and "bohemians" today. They worked in the streets and wore dresses fastened to one shoulder, which allowed them to be easily recognized. They approached passers-by and offered them their services in exchange for money.

**✳ The young man looks pretty self-assured.**
His elegance indicates that he is a member of the upper class; in addition to the sword—a privilege of the aristocracy—he wears clothes made of luxurious fabrics, and a hat embellished with superb feathers. Despite his very young age, the arrogance of his attitude with his hand on his hip reinforces the impression of self-confidence that he exudes. He seems hardly older than a teenager, but already looks quite proud of himself. He most likely considers that the material wealth he displays protects him from everything, thus exempting him from demonstrating any kind of wisdom or reason.

**✳ The fortune-teller is not looking at the young man's hand.**
She seems to be looking at the young man instead, as if she were watching him. He is not looking at her hand either, though she is discreetly sliding a ring from the hand of the elegant young man, who he is totally unaware of what she is doing! Indeed we see her two hooked fingers that seem to be gripping a ring in the gullible fool's palm.

**✳ Would the woman be a thief?**
She is stealing from the young man in two ways—by taking a jewel from him and by lying to him. For it is not certain that she can predict his future, even though he probably paid her to do so. On the other hand, this young man, arrogant though in fact rather inexperienced, seems to deserve a little lesson. The woman may not be the only guilty one in this particular tale!

✳ **Did artists often paint scenes portraying thieves?**
No... This was new at the time. Caravaggio was the first to paint pieces showing thieves and cheaters. This taste for portraying more accessible themes developed considerable during the 17th century —multiplying representations of the peasantry, of smoky tavern scenes... This was a reaction to the sophistication and the erudition of the arts in the 16th century. Realism blossomed particularly quickly in the Netherlands, where the Reformed Church did not favor the presence of religious paintings in their temples. Therefore, the painters, renouncing religious imagery, chose to practice a type of painting that depicted everyday life.
Although Italian, Caravaggio didn't hesitate to apply this new vision to classical themes, sometimes mixing popular characters with religious or mythological scenes. He was also much criticized for portraying the corpse of a lower class woman to represent the Virgin, in his work called *The Death of the Virgin*, displayed in this same gallery.

✳ **Weren't people shocked by such topics?**
In the painter's lifetime, using models from the general public to paint themes that belonged to *historical painting* (religious, historical or mythological themes—considered as noble) was hardly acceptable. On the other hand, *genre paintings* (everyday life topics) were particularly appreciated. Their moralizing topics were as many warnings against the consequences of a life unsettled by gambling, association with prostitutes, or drunkenness, which were far from the virtuous principles of simplicity, charity, or the love of study that the decent man was supposed to display.

✳ **For a scene taking place in the street, the characters are quite isolated!**
There are no elements actually suggesting the street. There is no façade, only two characters in front of a bare wall. Caravaggio customarily used compositions with tight framing of life-sized characters; he paid very little attention to the rest of the setting. This way, our attention is not diverted by secondary details and we are able to concentrate on the gestures and the feeling of movement created by the characters looks.
At the end of the 17th century, this painting was enlarged by about four inches at the top, probably in order to suit the current taste that favored wider and well-spaced framing of subject matter.

**Was Caravaggio a virtuous and wise man himself?**

Not at all... He had a tumultuous life and provoked numerous scandals similar to those of the realistic and popular characters depicted in some of his paintings. He was sent to prison several times for scuffling or making slanderous remarks about his colleague Giovanni Baglione. He was even prosecuted for a crime, committed during a brawl after a ball game. Sentenced to death by Pope Paul V, who wished to make an example of him, he had to leave Rome in 1606. He fled to Malta and later to Sicily.

**Was he recognized in his lifetime?**

Although his career was very short—he died at the age of 39—it revolutionized the world of painting. *The Fortune Teller* belongs to a series of paintings from the beginning of his career, favoring diurnal (day) lighting. But another part of his work, including *The Death of the Virgin*, is characterized by the use of *chiaroscuro*, a technique where parts of the canvas are highly lit while others are left in shadow.

Numerous painters all over Europe, such as Valentin de Boulogne or Georges de La Tour, would follow his example, depicting popular models and realistic scenes, inspired by his framing and lighting techniques, thereby creating a real new movement known as *Caravaggism*.

Despite their revolutionary character, his paintings could be found at the time in the collections of the greatest princes, such as that of the Duke of Mantua.

## *The Madonna of Chancellor Rolin*

1430-1434, oil on wood, 66 x 62 cm
Jan Van Eyck (Maasseyck, circa 1390/95 – Bruges, 1441)
Location: Richelieu, 2nd Floor- Paintings (Flanders)

**✳  Where does the scene take place?**

The characters are in a loggia, supported by Romanesque arch-
ways and opening onto a garden. In the garden we see a peacock
and magpies, as well as two characters with their backs to us.
Oddly enough, the garden looks as if it is situated on top of a fortress, since we can make out crenellations resembling those found
on a battlement. This strange place is located on building towers
above a city, which stretches along each bank of a river.
Supposedly, this city is Jerusalem. The artist is thus evoking two
worlds—the silent and protected world of the main scene, and the
open and dynamic world of the city below.

**✳  Is the painter portraying an existing landscape?**

The loggia setting is probably a vision from imagination, for it seems
highly unlikely to build an open loggia on top of a fortified tower.
However, the descriptions of some of the buildings in the background
seem so minutely detailed that historians have sometimes attempted
to identify them by name; for example, they believed they had recognized—above the child's head—the steeple of the Utrecht Cathedral...
It was not uncommon at the time to take inspiration from familiar
buildings, even when evoking such a remote city as Jerusalem, often
depicted with Venetian, Flemish, or Provencal architecture. More than
a real city, what we are talking about here is an idealized city as is
mentioned in the Apocalypse (Revelation of St. John the Divine)—
Heavenly Jerusalem, God's kingdom on earth.

**✳  What is the child doing?**

He is raising the two fingers of his right hand in a gesture of benediction. The crystal globe surmounted by a cross, sign of sovereignty over
the universe, as well as the gesture of benediction, indicate that this
is not just any child but the infant Jesus. The worried expression on
his face, marked by dark circles under his eyes, symbolizes the difficult destiny that awaits him—death by crucifixion.

**✳  Why is it there a small character holding a crown above the
woman's head?**

The woman is Mary, Jesus's mother, whose popularity was growing at
the end of the Middle Ages. This explains the honored place she was
given in this painting. She is usually shown being crowned by Christ, or
sometimes, as here, by an angel. The angel, feminine in appearance is
recognizable by its wings. Angels are in fact asexual characters.

Notwithstanding the setting and the age of Jesus, the action of the angel crowning the Madonna, tells us that Mary and the Child are not depicted during their terrestrial life. Here, the Madonna represents the queen of Heavenly Jerusalem, the city suggested by the landscape.

### ✴ Who was the Chancellor Rolin?

Nicolas Rolin was chancellor to the Duke of Burgundy, Philip the Good. Being a chancellor meant being the Keeper of the Seals—hence, of the Duke's signature. Nicolas Rolin was a very powerful minister, for, in those days, the Dukedom also included Flanders. The Duke was a very wealthy man and commissioned the Dukedom's greatest artists, such as Jan Van Eyck, the author of this work. The painting was intended for his funerary chapel, in the church of Notre Dame du Châtel, in Autun—no longer in existence. Rolin was also, with his wife, founder of the famous Beaune Hospices.

### ✴ Is the chancellor looking at the Madonna?

He is not looking at her, for she is not physically in front of him. He is kneeling in prayer and he "sees" her through his prayer. Also note that no one's line of vision in the painting crosses another.

### ✴ What do the sculpted scenes above the chancellor's head portray?

On the *capitals* (the wider section on top of a column), you can identify different Bible stories. From left to right—Adam and Eve chased from heaven, Abel's murder, Noah's drunkenness. Far from being chosen casually, these three scenes, taken from the Old Testament, along with the Romanesque arches—which were out of fashion when the painting was executed—express the transition between the old world and the new one, incarnated by Christ. Numerous details that may first seem of minor interest are actually rich in religious significance. The garden lilies, and the notion of protection conveyed by the fortress, suggest the purity of the Madonna. The peacock evokes immortality promised to the disciples of Christ, while small rabbits—symbolizing the concept of lust—are squashed by columns...

### ✴ This picture is painted very realistically.

In spite of the symbolical nature of the scene, the painter endeavored to minutely detail the different textures, suggesting the luxuriousness of fabrics, the veins in the floor's marble tile, the light coming through the stained glassed windows above the central arch, the delicacy of the crown's metal work and many others...

Particular attention is paid to the realism of Nicolas Rolin's face—we can distinguish his scruffy beard, the wrinkles which mark his features...

Jan Van Eyck was also interested in how space was represented. Perspective is created and perceived not only through the vanishing lines of the floor tiles but also by the softening of the background colors, which suggest distance. Many other artists will later use the second technique, which is known as "atmospheric perspective" (for example Leonardo da Vinci in his *Mona Lisa* landscape).

✳ **Jan Van Eyck liked to paint reflections.**

Jan Van Eyck—the most famous Flemish painter of his time—was renowned for the quality in the treatment of light in his paintings. He multiplied details in order to render the play of light on the crown, the border of the Madonna's dress, the brocade on the chancellor's coat, the stained-glass window or the river...

The colors are not simply juxtaposed without concern for the unity of light; their tonalities vary according to their position in the painting's composition. Thus, the artist describes different types of lighting for the interior (darker and favorable to contemplation) and the exterior (brighter). He was also said to have invented oil-based paint, that's more suitable for subtle color work than egg-based tempera paint, which had been used so far. Among other techniques, it's oil-based paint that allowed Leonardo da Vinci to obtain such nuanced contours for *Mona Lisa*'s face.

✳ **Is it true that Jan Van Eyck was valet for the Duke of Burgundy?**

Yes it is true, but, mind you, this was a highly honorable position, since it was equivalent to that of a diplomat and not a servant! As a member of the Duke's court, he was sometimes sent on secret missions, which could involve such things as negotiations for a princely wedding—the painter being led to execute a portrait of the duke's potential fiancée. As court painter, he received an annual salary, which kept him from suffering the irregularities of commissions. His singular status, his style and his interest in new techniques make him—like Leonardo da Vinci—one of the characteristic painters of the Renaissance, a period which began simultaneously in Flanders and Italy (albeit in different forms) in the 15th century.

## The Ship of Fools

Around 1500, oil on wood, 58 x 33 cm
Jheronymus Bosch Van Aken, known as Hieronymus Bosch (Bois-le-Duc, circa 1450 – *idem*, 1516)
Location: Richelieu, 2nd Floor - Painting (Flanders)

* **Where are all these characters located?**
  They are stuck on a ship, one without a helm or a sail. This means that none of the characters on board can navigate it. The boat is sailing aimlessly, drifting along with the ever-changing current.

* **What are they doing?**
  They are eating and drinking to excess. As you can see, there's even a sick man vomiting on the right side of the painting. Just to his left, another man climbs up the ship's mast in order to catch a bird. Another man and a woman seem to be fighting over a wine pitcher. The characters in the center are trying to bite into a crepe that is suspended from a string.

* **It almost resembles a fairground!**
  Indeed, the artist composed this scene keeping in mind the different types of entertainment that cities offered in his day on the occasional holiday—catching a crepe without using your hands, testing your agility by climbing a greasy pole to grab hold of a hanging prize... These games were similar to the games of chance and other competitions that are played during our modern day fairs.

* **Why place these individuals on a boat?**
  At the time, "fools" or lunatics were often pictured in helmless ships in order to symbolize their fickleness. They drift along, flowing on the current of their fancy and their odd habits, living for the moment without thinking about the future. Here, they are indulging in gluttony with no concern for the consequences. Bosch was probably inspired by the book *The Ship of Fools*, in which the author, Sebastian Brandt, imagined a world that was like a ship loaded with fools or madmen, drifting towards *Naragonia* (fools' paradise).

* **What an odd theme!**
  On the right, the character sitting on a branch is wearing the traditional fool's costume. He has got small bells hanging from his waist, and is holding a ridiculous scepter called a "fool's bauble" (a puppet's head being considered the attribute of madness) on which figures a mask with a long pointy hat fastened to a wooden-stick. Bosch's model is the fool from the princely courts—a character whose role was that of jester and who was authorized to address the sovereign with great insolence. The other characters are wearing ordinary clothes.

In fact, the artist is not attacking real fools but rather some of his contemporaries who, as they indulged in excess, turned away from God. With this painting, his intention was to denounce the moral failings of his fellow men. It is a visual metaphor—here, lunacy is synonym for vice and sin. It is a warning against the consequences of the two vices, gluttony and drunkenness.

❋ **A monk and a nun!**
Since they are in the foreground, you can't miss them. The nun is holding a lute that creates a highlighted spot that catches the eye. It was a time when people were beginning to denounce the behavior of certain members of the clergy for their ignorance and their extravagant behavior. By the way, these excesses committed by the clergy created turmoil that led to the Reformation—that is to say, to the creation of a new branch of Christianity (Protestant), independent from the Pope's authority which was judged as too corrupt. The new Protestant churches developed particularly in northern European countries, including Holland, where our painter lived.

❋ **Did he paint other pictures as striking as this one?**
Yes. He was quite famous for his topics describing eccentricities as well as vices—for instance, *The Seven Deadly* Sins (exhibited in Madrid) or *The Temptation of Saint Anthony*, a pretext for depicting a crowd of monsters figuring the devil (in Lisbon).
In reality, this panel is a fragment from a triptych, which became separated over the years. The central part has never been found; the right panel, portraying the death of a miser, is exhibited in Washington. It seems therefore, that the ensemble treated at least two sins—miserliness and gluttony.
In addition, we know that the panel currently housed by the Louvre was originally taller, since there exists a smaller panel exhibited at Yale University in the United States. This smaller piece fits perfectly with the lower section of the *Ship of Fools*. It was unfortunately rather frequent to see panels cut into pieces, for the sake of the art trade, with several museums keeping a section of each.

**✳ Bosch liked to paint ugliness.**
At the time, a painting was not merely a decorative object for collection. It was also a support either for prayer or for meditation. Therefore, although they were often filled with caricatured and ugly characters, Bosch's paintings seduced his contemporaries who were fond in art thought-provoking themes.

**✳ What did his contemporaries think about such paintings?**
Despite the strange topics of his paintings, Bosch was not at all a marginal character. He was well integrated in his Dutch town of Bois Le Duc and valued as an artist by collectors and kings. Indeed, after the death of the artist, Philip II, King of Spain, bought a number of his paintings, which can still be seen today at the Prado in Madrid.

**✳ Was he the only one to paint this kind of subjects?**
He was the first in a long line of Northern European artists to use scenes from everyday life in order to denounce men's vices. But his manner of treating these subjects was quite innovative at the time. His technique, made up of small, thick and visible strokes was in stark contrast with the very smooth and precise styles of the artists who preceded him.

## Self-Portrait

1493, oil on parchment mounted on canvas, 56 x 44 cm
Albrecht Dürer (Nuremberg, 1471 – idem, 1528)
Location: Richelieu, 2nd Floor - Painting (Germany)

✳ **This man doesn't appear very natural.**
That's because he is posing for this painting. His body is turned towards the left, but his eyes are looking to the right. In his hands he holds a thistle blossom. Considering the time required to execute this painting, he may have remained in this position for hours.

✳ **It looks as if he is looking at somebody.**
This is a self-portrait; that is to say that the artist painted his own image by studying his reflection in a mirror. Only the concentrated look of his eyes allows us to guess that he is at the same time the model and the painter, since he didn't include either the brushes or the *palette* (the wooden board used to hold and mix colors) that he was necessarily using.

✳ **Isn't he wearing a rather elegant outfit for painting?**
In the 15th century, you could determine which social group (aristo-cracy, artisans, clergy...) a person belonged to by looking at the clothes they wore. Clothes were highly codified and the codes were strictly respected. In this way, you could easily know with whom you were dealing. Here, Dürer did not wish to portray himself in an artisan's costume, although he belonged to the artisans' class. In this painting, he wears the costume of an aristocrat.

✳ **Why didn't he portray himself as a painter?**
It may have been that he didn't wish to show his profession, in order to assert his ambitions. He was very young when he executed this painting and was only just beginning his career. He had to prove him-self to others. The painting was probably intended for his fiancée, who came from a higher social background. The richness of his clothing shows the wealth he aspires to and, hence, the confidence he has in his talent. He probably sensed that his skill would allow him to mix with or join the bourgeoisie and the aristocracy. And indeed, it was in these milieus that he would come to find his principal clients—notably among bankers and sovereigns, such as Frederic the Wise, Elector of Saxony, Emperor Maximilian or Charles V. He would eventually come under the protection of the great politicians of the Holy Roman Empire, from which he received a pension.

✳ **Holding a thistle seems like a strange idea.**
Numerous portraits feature an attribute making reference to a pro-fession or to an era's known code. The thistle (*eryngium maritimum* or sea holly) symbolized fidelity. Away in Strasbourg at the time he

**109**

painted this picture, the artist—a young and attractive man—sent, via this painting, a message of fidelity to the woman he was engaged to and who had remained behind, in their home town of Nuremberg. This canvas thus became an instrument for his long-distance courtship. The portrait was painted on *parchment* (ox skin), allowing it to be rolled up and to travel more easily.

✳ **He must have been a very proud person to represent himself in such a way.**
Considered mere craftsmen, painters placed their works in the forefront, not signing them. This explains why numerous artists of past centuries are unknown to us and why we can't always be certain about the identity of a painting's creator. In this case, a piece will be marked "attributed to," in order to signify that we have strong presumptions as to who painted it, but that we can't say this with 100% certainty.
As for Dürer, he was aware of his own value as an artist and he proclaimed it in two ways—first by executing a self-portrait, and second by appending his signature (his monogram: AD) at the top of the painting.

✳ **Why did he sign his painting?**
In Dürer's lifetime, the status of painters was evolving. As of the 15th century, people were no longer buying a painting according to the topic it depicted, but also according to the artist's fame—a fame that resulted from, among other things, the artist's individual talent. The notion of art, as we perceive it today, substituted itself for the older notions of arts and crafts. Aware of their newly found importance, artists began claiming their own creative originality and began choosing themselves as subject matter for their work. It was a way for them to assert their position in society as well as their role as creators. To own a painting by a renowned artist was important; to own a self-portrait by a renowned artist would be considered a privilege for a long time to come.
Nevertheless, Dürer didn't fail to recall his own humility by adding a phrase in German above his portrait: "Things with me fare as ordained from above"...

✳ **When did artists begin signing their works?**
The presence of a signature was still rare in the 16th century and remains quite a random event in following centuries. Until the 19th century, those commissioning work entered into direct contact with the artist—they didn't need a signature that would authenticate the

**110**

painting's author. However, the development of the art market and the multiplication of middlemen, such as art galleries and dealers created a distance between the artist and the client. This sometimes led to a bidding war for artworks; collectors would then demand proof of the creator's identity, his signature being the best evidence.

## ✳ What if the painting is not signed?

It can also be marked "from the studio of," which meant that it was executed in the master's workshop, although not necessarily by the master's hand. As a matter of fact, there were assistants working in the style of the workshop's master on his behalf.

As for the term "school of," this indicates a stylistic relationship, without relaying the certitude that the work was indeed executed in the master's studio. The painting was executed by someone referred to as an "imitator."

## ✳ Did Dürer often paint self-portraits?

We know of three self-portraits drawn and executed previous to this first painted self-portrait, among which, one was painted at the age of 13. Later on, Dürer would consistently represent himself in his paintings. Sometimes his image would be an isolated self-portrait, like the one at the Louvre; sometimes he would hide it in a religious scene, like in the *Adoration of the Magi*, to be found in Florence.

## ✳ Was his talent recognized as he had hoped?

Yes... He was a renowned artist in his lifetime, notably for his talent as an engraver. His engravings were easily reproducible, which allowed them to circulate more readily than his paintings. His first series of important engravings were based on the biblical theme of the Apocalypse and had great success throughout Europe. This is quite something when you take into consideration that at the time there was a total absence of rapid means of communication.

## ✳ Did Dürer travel a lot?

Traveling was an important part of any artist's training. The painter had to meet with other creators and observe how they worked. Curious about everything, like many enlightened minds of his time, Dürer traveled in Germany, but also in Flanders (Belgium and Holland) as well as in Italy, to Venice.

Today, we can still see many of his *watercolors*. Painted during his foreign travels, they constitute a veritable album, just like the photos that we bring back from our own travels today.

## The Meeting at Lyon

1621-1625, oil on canvas, 3.94 x 2.95 m
Petrus Paulus, known as Peter Paul Rubens (Siegen, 1577 – Antwerp, 1640)
Location: Richelieu, 2nd Floor - Painting (Flanders) – Galerie Médicis

18

✱ **It's full of animals.**
Yes... Actually, you can make out three different species and all of them have a symbolic function—they help us recognize what the painter wished to represent. Thus, on the right part of the canvas, the eagle is the attribute of Jupiter, king of the Roman gods. He is also identified by the lightning bolt that he holds in his left hand, reminding us that he is the god of lightning and thunder. The long-tailed peacock is the attribute of Juno, Jupiter's wife. As for the lions, they give the name to the city of Lyon, where the scene takes place.

✱ **Who is the woman in the chariot drawn by the lions?**
She is an allegory, just like the two women in Titian's *Concert Champêtre*. She personifies the city of Lyon, which is also represented in the landscape on the left section of the background. It was customary to symbolize a city by a woman wearing a crown made up of towers resembling a fortification. These representations sometimes appear in the shape of statues. You can see some of them on the Place de la Concorde (representing the cities of Nantes, Lille, Lyon, Marseille, Bordeaux...) not far from the Louvre. There are others in train stations, where they indicate the destinations served by the trains.

✱ **Some characters are sitting on clouds!**
The characters are rising up into the air, which proves that these are no ordinary people—they are the King and Queen of France, Henri IV and Marie de Medici. Their images are deified because they are portrayed as Jupiter and Juno. This is a *mythological portrait* (a representation of an individual with a god's attributes) that allowed the artist to portray Marie de Medici with a bare breast, in spite of the fact that she was the daughter of the Great Duke of Tuscany.

✱ **Why is Henry IV taking her hand?**
The painting celebrates the two spouses' first meeting. The painter wanted to convey the king's deference towards his wife—he steps over his eagle with great haste, to come to her. Nevertheless, this was not a union of love but a contractual one. Marie de Medici had married the king by proxy on 5 October 1660. This union, which had actually been arranged in order to bail out the French royal treasure, thanks to the fiancée's dowry, was celebrated in Florence, Tuscany, even though king Henry IV was not present. The king, busy with state affairs, and his affair with Henriette d'Entragues, had himself represented by diplomats who negotiated the union on his behalf.

**113**

**✳ Who is the woman holding a flaming torch?**

Hymen, the mythological goddess of marriage. Her position, over-hanging the scene, the benevolent look on her face and her pro-tective position indicate that she is taking care of the new royal couple's future. The rainbow on the upper left side also evokes celestial protection from which these nuptials will benefit, as they are to bring prosperity to the kingdom. The *putti*, angels incar-nated by nude children, behind Jupiter and the lions, reinforce Hymen with the torches that they are brandishing.

**✳ Who ordered this painting?**

This painting is part of an ensemble of twenty-four paintings com-missioned by Marie de Medici from Rubens for the Luxembourg Palace. The construction of this residence—the present-day seat of the French Senate—was commissioned so that she wouldn't have to dwell at the Louvre, which was the centre of France's power after the wedding of her son, King Louis XIII. These art-works composed a gallery in praise of the Queen Mother's life and political action. After the death of Henri IV in 1610, she undertook the Regency until Louis XIII came of age.

Unlike the Galerie d'Apollon at the Louvre, where the ceilings and walls are also decorated, the Medici Gallery in the Luxembourg Palace was only decorated with wall hangings, today entirely pre-served and displayed in the Louvre.

**✳ Why move this collection to the Louvre?**

The room which first displayed the paintings in their entirety was altered in 1800; stairs were added and the paintings were moved to another gallery in Luxembourg Palace, before transfer to the Louvre in 1815.

**✳ Why was a Flemish painter commissioned to decorate the gallery?**

Flemish, yes, but above all, he was the most famous painter of the day. Peter Paul Rubens was a sought-after and prolific painter, working for the church as well as for the courts of Italy, France, England and Spain. There was no other French artist decorator in the early century who would have been capable of achieving such a large-scale ensemble, measuring nearly a thousand square-feet. The most promising ones, such as Simon Vouet, were still training in Italy while Rubens had reached full maturity and, thereby, international fame.

✳ **Did Rubens paint it all by himself?**
Yes... The queen insisted that the totality of the twenty-four canvases be painted by Rubens's own hand. This was exceptional,
since usually when studio masters were confronted with such a
commission, they would prepare the subject with sketches or
models and then leave the execution of the final piece to their
assistants.

✳ **How long did it take to paint the entire gallery?**
The whole job took him four years, which is not long, if you
consider the extent of the task that had to be single-handedly
achieved. It is true that the techniques used here were far from
being as precise as Jan Van Eyck's for example. On account of the
dimensions, Rubens used broad brushes that were suitable for the
size he was dealing with. He found it useless to minutely paint
details that couldn't be seen from afar. Shapes were suggested by
broad strokes and creamy textures that you can only perceive when
close to the paintings.

# Bathsheba

1654, oil on canvas, 1.42 x 1.42 m
Rembrandt Harmenszoon Van Rijn, known as Rembrandt (Leiden, 1606 – Amsterdam, 1669)
Location: Richelieu, 2$^{nd}$ Floor - Painting (Holland)

19

**★ There are not many colors.**
Rembrandt always used the same palette of colors, composed mainly of varied gradations of browns, yellows and beiges, called *monochromes*. On this canvas, only the floor and the ribbon in the woman's hair are red.

**★ In which room of the house are we?**
The bed placed in the background evokes a bedroom or a private chamber. This is thus an intimate scene.

**★ The room is not well lit.**
The characters in Rembrandt's paintings always look as if they were coming out of shadow. Some details are brightly lit, such as the young woman's naked body, or the white linen she is leaning on; others are very somber, such as the wall above the bed. Here, the light may be coming from a window on the upper left corner. There is also a bit of light coming from a room located behind the nude woman.

**★ Why does the she look so sad?**
This woman, Bathsheba, is holding a letter which, according to art historians' differing versions, either summons her to King David, or recounts very bad news—the death of her husband Uriah. Uriah had been sent to war by King David who desired his death. As a matter of fact, David had fallen in love with Bathsheba after catching a glimpse of her coming out of her bath. By depicting her nude with the missive in her hand, the artist not only combines two different moments of the story, but also lets us understand why David fell in love.

**★ Who is the old woman on the left?**
She is Bathsheba's servant. She wipes her lady's feet, thus evoking the idea of a bath even though we do not see a bathtub. Her old age helps the painter to highlight Bathsheba's youth.

**★ Where does this story come from?**
This is a story told in the Bible's Old Testament, which Rembrandt had often studied and from which he often took inspiration.

### ✳ Was the painting intended for a church?

No... Although based on a religious theme, this painting was intended for a collector. In Holland, Rembrandt's country, where the majority of people were Protestants, it was not an accepted practice to decorate places of worship with artworks. Religious paintings were thus intended for private interiors.

### ✳ Why did she keep her jewels while bathing?

In fact, the theme of Bathsheba was merely a pretext to paint a female nude. In the 17th century, it was not conceivable to paint a naked woman. Therefore, in order to get around this moral interdiction, artists would use the pretext of legends from antiquity or from the Bible, in order to treat the theme of the nude. The tales of Bathsheba or Venus were often used in this manner.

### ✳ Bathsheba looks real enough and she's not beautiful!

Rembrandt depicts her with a slightly thick body. She definitely doesn't correspond to the current standards of beauty but in Rembrandt's time, she must have been considered quite lovely.
This painting is also an intimate portrait, for the painter's model is the woman he was in love with at the time, Hendrickje Stoffels. She actually posed for him quite often. Sometimes, Rembrandt also painted his son under the guise of an angel. It is not rare, even today, that artists take inspiration from their close relations in creating their works.

### ✳ Wasn't it shocking to pose nude?

At the time, moral codes forbade women to pose nude for a man. Women's clothes would cover their bodies almost entirely; you couldn't show your legs or arms at will during the day. Women who revealed their bodies, who wore low-cut dress—like Franz Hals's *Gipsy Girl* on display in the same department—were considered shameless hussies. Women were in charge of the education of children and were to adopt virtuous and modest attitudes and appearance, to which their clothing attested.
This explains why artists would use their close relations as models. It was more discrete. Nevertheless, nude paintings were scarce in Holland, and on this account, this painting is exceptional. Rembrandt didn't much care about possible gossip. A rather free painter, he was in the middle of his career and didn't grant much importance to critics.

* **The paint is quite thick in some places.**
  When looking at the fabrics, the brush strokes are clearly visible. Rembrandt didn't dilute his pigments very much, which gave them a somewhat creamy consistency and which translates visually the fabrics's material. In this way, he helps us to feel the material's texture with our eyes. Rembrandt knew that the eye recognizes a subject not only by the shape of its contours and its color, but also by its texture. His technique was at odds with that used by his contemporaries, who would look to make a precise sketch and paint a slick surface. To some, Rembrandt's paintings must have seemed rather "botched."

* **The canvas is square**
  Painters rarely resorted to using such a format that, like circular formats, is slightly more difficult to work with. However, the square shape adapts perfectly to Bathsheba's body. The whole painting is conceived as a showcase for the female form—the square shape underlines the body's proportions; the lustrous bronze shade of the bed's fabric enhances the paleness of her skin; the impastos (thick color strokes) form a contrast with the more blended strokes of Bathsheba's flesh. This is a beautiful homage from the artist to the woman he loved.

## The Astronomer

1668, oil on canvas, 51 x 45 cm
Johannes Vermeer (Delft, 1632 – idem, 1675)
Location: Richelieu, 2nd Floor - Painting (Holland)

20

* **It is a rather small painting.**
  It was intended for a private interior, of a size more modest than a palace. In Holland, where this canvas was painted, you could find paintings in almost every class of society. Some of Vermeer's paintings are even said to have belonged to a baker.

* **Why is the man wearing a long coat in his home?**
  This man lived in a quite cold land. The houses were not well heated; it was necessary to wear warm clothes even inside. You can often see, in Dutch paintings of the era, women wearing jackets lined with fur.

* **He looks concentrated.**
  He is at work in his office. He has a book opened in front of him and is observing motifs on a globe that he seems to be spinning with his hand. In Holland, men were often represented reflecting, or working in their studies.

* **The tablecloth covering his desk is too big!**
  It's a carpet, not a tablecloth. In the 17th century, carpets were not only intended to decorate the floors, they also covered tables; this practice is attested to in Dutch painting from this era. This carpet can't be very useful, but it creates a kind of decorative effect gladly sought after by painters. The slightly velvety texture of the carpet is precisely rendered with the help of small brush strokes. The pleats create large shaded areas that contrast with the brightly lit objects in the background. The whole picture is painted with extreme accuracy.

* **The globe is particularly highlighted.**
  It benefits from light coming from the window. Its wooden stand, situated at the painting's halfway point, is precisely on the level of the windowsill. The man's hand and eyes lead us to look straight at the globe. It seems evident that it is an important element of the painting.

✴ **The motifs on the globe are rather strange.**
These are fabulous animals, mythological characters used to evoke the constellations. This globe doesn't actually materialize the earth but the heavens. The objects scattered around it are all linked to the study of astronomy: the astrolabe, half hidden by the carpet, was used by sailors to navigate by the stars; the book, painted so minutely that it was possible to identify it, is a manual of astronomy written by Adrian Metius.

✴ **Did Vermeer possess all the depicted objects?**
Like many Dutch painters, Vermeer liked to paint everyday life. The objects most likely belonged to him and the room itself was probably one of the rooms in his own house—the window and the picture hanging on the wall on the right can be identified in other works of his.

✴ **Why did he place his desk by the window?**
This position was ideal for taking advantage of the natural light. Before the invention of electricity, you had to make the most of available light sources. Vermeer uses this quite rational arrangement to express his talent—he takes particular care in showing us the variations of light on the globe or the reflections on metal objects. He even painted the reflection of the astrolabe on the wall just below the window, a spot that would normally be difficult for daylight to reach.

✴ **Do we know who the model is?**
No... Some have proclaimed that this is a self-portrait, but there is no information to prove this. More than a man, Vermeer relished in depicting a science—astronomy—as well as in demonstrating his talent in recreating light and textures. Astronomy was very important for the Dutch, a sailing people, who navigated the seas thanks to their knowledge of the stars.

✴ **Why are there letters on the cupboard?**
This is the date, written in Roman numerals. It is believed to indicate when the painting was executed. You can also make out a inscription difficult to read, just above it (IV Meer) which could be the painter's signature. Dates and signatures are rather rare in Vermeer's work. It is important to know this kind of information in order to better understand an artist's style and evolution—hence the interest of this painting exhibited in the Louvre.

**※ Did Vermeer paint this canvas for himself?**

It is not likely. Most of the painters at that time worked on commission. Even though the piece represents elements from the artist's home, the painting was intended for a collector.

**※ Was Vermeer a prolific painter?**

There are not many Vermeers in existence. He was a demanding painter and probably didn't paint much more than the thirty-two pieces we know of today. He was also an art dealer, but it was not rare in Holland at the time that a painter would hold several different jobs just to make a living.

## The Villeneuve-lès-Avignon Pietà

Around 1455, oil on wood, 1.63 x 2.18 m
Enguerrand Quarton (native of Laon Diocese, known in Provence 1444-66)
Location: Richelieu, 2nd Floor - Painting (France)

21

✳ **Why do the characters appear so sad?**
Lying on the lap of the woman in the middle of the painting, a man has passed away; his body bears the traces of wounds.

✳ **Who are they?**
The man lying down is Christ. He was taken down from the cross on which he died. He was then laid down on his mother's, the Virgin Mary's, lap. To their right, Mary Magdalene wipes her eyes with her garment and holds a bottle that permits us to identify her; the story has it that she had washed Jesus's feet with perfume coming from a bottle, during a prior meal that they had shared. To the left, John, one of Jesus's companions, is delicately holding Christ's head to remove the crown of thorns that had been placed there in mockery. Each character's name is written in the halo that encircles their head.

✳ **What about the fifth character?**
This is the donor, the one who commissioned the painting. The man stands apart; he doesn't belong to the same world as the other characters and doesn't have a halo. He is not looking at the scene but gazing far away into the void. The man's face is quite dry and marked with wrinkles; the tip of his nose is red and his hair is not well combed. Small, disheveled locks stick out here and there. His white outfit allows us to identify him as a Carthusian monk, but we don't know his name. He is praying, showing us what 15th century people would do upon viewing this painting, which was at the time displayed in a church, the Carthusian monnastery of Villeneuve-lès-Avignon. In fact, the painting's central scene is the materialization of images from his prayer.

✳ **There's something written on the painting.**
All around the golden background, you can read a phrase in Latin. The translation would be "Look and see if there exists a pain such as mine." The Virgin might be saying this, for she is mourning and grieving her son's death.

✳ **It feels like the donor is hearing the words.**
Indeed, his ear is oddly raised, as if he were lending an ear to these supplications. Besides, it was certainly not a coincidence if the painter chose to set the sentence's first word in proximity to the donor's ear.

✳ **What is the city in the background?**
It is Jerusalem, where Jesus was crucified. The painter, who most likely never traveled there, painted buildings with domes, in order to evoke a Middle Eastern city. He may have taken inspiration from engravings made by other artists, who had accomplished this far and difficult journey. These engravings, which were in circulation at the time in artists' studios, helped enrich the visual repertory that painters had at their disposal.

✳ **Christ's body seems very stiff!**
The painter doesn't just symbolize death by Christ's outstretched body; he actually makes a visual description of a corpse. He insists on the body's stiffness through the position of the right arm and the hollow of Christ's back. The green color of his flesh and the blood that had flowed from the dried up wound, are also very realistic.

✳ **The artist has a taste for detail.**
If you take a closer look, you can see tears running down Mary Magdalene's cheek. You can also see drops of liquid still flowing from Christ's dead body.

✳ **The painting is damaged.**
This painting is more than five hundred years old and the colors have slightly altered. The paint used for Mary Magdalene's coat is worn, but this defect allows us to see the base sketch underneath the color. You can also make out some red coloring resurfacing beneath the worn out gold of the sky. This is the base used for fixing gold leaf.

✳ **The painting looks as if it were painted on planks.**
Like Giotto's *Saint Francis of Assisi Receiving the Stigmata*, the support for this painting is actually wood, an unstable material. This is how you can clearly see that the support of the work was made up of unequally wide pieces, which have moved since they were first assembled in the 15th century.

* **The painting is centered on the Madonna.**
  *Pietà* is the term we use when talking about the representation of the Virgin Mary's grief at the death of her son. This is the moment when she accepts his death and prays. The holy characters form a triangular block whose point corresponds to the emplacement of Mary's head; thus she is at the center of the composition. Her hands joined in prayer are directly in line with the painting. This is how the artist reveals the painting's first purpose—an invitation to prayer.

## Francis I, King of France (1494-1547)

Around 1530, oil on wood, 96 x 74 cm
Jean Clouet (?, 1485/1490 – ? 1540/1541)
Location: Richelieu, 2nd Floor - Painting (France)

22

**★ He looks like an American football player!**

Indeed, this is the impression given by his outfit, which is so big it doesn't seem to fit into the painting's space. He is wearing a really luxurious garment with large, flared sleeves that was fashionable in the 16th century. Of course, only the wealthiest people could afford to wear clothes that required so much fabric. There's even gold woven into them!

**★ His eyes look like they are following us.**

He seems to be scrutinizing the people that are around him  His face is turned to one side, while his eyes are looking the other way. By posing this way, he looks like he is observing us, wherever we may be in the room. This is an effect that conveys power, majesty and perhaps mistrust.

**★ Is he a French king?**

On the fabric covering the wall behind him, on the right, a crown indicates that we are actually in presence of a king. Even though he is not wearing his crown, as we see in other royal portraits, it is still perfectly visible.

**★ Is this good a portrait of him?**

This is Francis I, King of France, who had notably invited Leonardo da Vinci to his demeure in Amboise. Like all kings, he enjoyed having his portrait painted, and the Louvre owns another portrait of him, displayed nearby in the same department. You can easily recognize him when comparing the two paintings—rather small eyes, a long nose, thin lips. In this portrait, the sovereign is painted life-size. He was very tall, almost six and a half feet. You can guess this by looking at the breadth of his neck and shoulders. It is almost as if he were right here before us.

**★ What's that strange thing the King has on his head?**

He is wearing a beret, embellished with feathers and down. The hat blends with his mid-length hair, which is hiding his ears. There isn't a lock of hair out of place.

## ✳ The hands look unfinished

They look a bit blurry, indeed. The nails are not flawlessly drawn. The hands form a contrast with the finely rendered details of the face and its precision. It is not certain that the same man executed the whole piece. There is a possibility that François Clouet, son of Jean, helped execute this portrait. This would explain the differences in the style. It was quite frequent that two artists would collaborate on a same painting. The son could then relieve the father from part of his workload.

## ✳ Where is he?

This is difficult to determine. It looks like he's in a theater-box. In front of the king, we can make out the edge of a balcony covered by green shiny fabric. One thing is certain though—King Francis I is not surprised by the painter's presence; the pomp and circumstance of his pose have been cleverly thought out in order to make a grand impression.

## ✳ The surface of the painting is slick and shiny.

The painter used a very meticulous technique. Each hair of his beard was reproduced with a very fine brush. The details of the embroideries are rendered with precision. Small drops of color were used to evoke the reflections on the gold and the fabrics. It takes a long time to obtain a painting displaying such perfection in the rendering of details.

## ✳ Did the king pose for this painting?

He posed at least for an initial sketch, which in the Musée Condé in Chantilly. Occupied with state affairs, a king was obviously not available to dedicate the time needed for the execution of a portrait. Consequently, artists would only hold a few posing sessions with their model, during which they would make sketches. A painting's conception would come from these sketches. If needed, they would use other models for the final attitudes.

## ✳ What is the purpose of a king's portrait?

Throughout history, influential men have had representations made of themselves in order to display their power. Here the monnarch wears a necklace of the religious order of Saint Michael, which he led. In the medallion, a scene pictures the saint fighting a dragon; beneath the king's left hand we see a sword handle. Only knights were allowed to carry a sword.

**❋ Was Francis 1$^{st}$ an important king for the French?**
Besides his political action, he was of great importance to the arts. He invited Italian artists to renovate Fontainebleau castle (e.g. Primatice or Rosso), thus introducing the Italian Renaissance in France. He commissioned the prestigious Château de Chambord. He also decided to have the medieval fortress of the Louvre destroyed and replaced by a more modern and luxurious building. By doing so, he launched the construction of the palace in which the museum is established today.

**❋ Was he really as powerful as he looks?**
Not at the time this picture was painted. A few years earlier, he had been imprisoned in Spain and had to renounce some of the territories over which he had previously reigned.
But the portrait is not meant to respect historical truth. A veritable communication tool, this official image was above all intended to convey the idea of royal power.

# *Christ in the Carpenter's Shop*

Around 1642, oil on canvas, 1.37 x 1.02 m
Georges de La Tour (Vic-sur-Seille, 1593 – Lunéville, 1652)
Location: Sully, 2nd Floor - Painting (France)

23

★ **It is so dark!**
The characters are plunged into obscurity. It may be nighttime. A seated child carries a candle in order to light the way for an old man.

★ **What is the old man doing?**
He is drilling a hole in a wooden beam. You can make out carpenter's tools on the floor—an auger, which resembles a kind of large corkscrew, used to drill the hole, a wooden sledgehammer and a wood chisel on the lower edge of the canvas.

★ **The characters are dressed simply.**
Their clothing is representative of modest people from the 17th century. Their clothes show their status as craftsmen. The man wears an apron on top of a shirt and a pair of pants that stop at the knee; the child is wearing a dress with a red belt.

★ **Why paint craftsmen?**
It may not look like it, but this is a religious painting, almost certainly intended for a church. The man is Joseph and the child is Jesus. Nevertheless, we don't see the halos that we normally associate with religious paintings which identify sacred characters. The artist chose to portray them performing the tasks of everyday life, without adding any distinctive marks. It may have been his attempt to reach the faithful more directly, by treating a religious scene in a more familiar manner, one closer to their everyday life.

★ **Jesus looks like a little girl!**
Similar to the Virgin from the Sainte Chapelle, the artist depicted the infant Jesus simply like any other child of the day, with long hair and a short tunic. This makes it even more difficult for us to identify the subject today!

★ **You can't see the setting.**
The scene concentrates on the characters, which fill up the whole canvas space. The old man's body is framed by two of the painting's edges, giving the impression that he is enclosed in a box. Only the highlighted faces contrast sharply with the obscurity of the background; this is a beautiful example of chiaroscuro painting.

**✳ Is it very difficult to paint light like this?**

Yes it is. Georges de La Tour executed a great number of paintings in which the study of candle or torch light is of prime importance. These are called *nocturnes* or nights. A real virtuoso in the treatment of light, he describes with great accuracy the slightly pinkish transparency of the child's hand protecting the flame from the gusts of wind. Jesus's very smooth cheek contrasts with the thicker strokes underlining Joseph's wrinkles.

**✳ There's only one wood shaving!**

It is true that one single wood shaving in a carpenter's workshop doesn't seem very realistic. Yet, Georges de La Tour was not looking to recreate the laborious atmosphere of the workshop with exactitude. A single shaving was enough to suggest Joseph's craft and, with a few strokes of thicker color, the artist expresses its volume and lighting. This apparently insignificant detail, placed in the foreground, was extremely difficult to achieve, and a beautiful example of the painter's technical mastery. This thin wooden ribbon constitutes the unnecessary and luxurious virtuosity of a master in full possession of his craft.

**✳ How do you know that it is a religious scene?**

We know this is a religious scene because of the unusual light. We do not have the impression that the flame from the candle illuminates the Child, but that the light actually radiates from his own face, as if it were illuminated from inside. This gives him a supernatural quality. At the time, Jesus was often compared to a new light shining over the world. In addition, he is the one holding the candle and, literally, lighting Joseph's way.

**✳ Are the characters talking?**

It's hard to tell. The child's mouth is slightly open and he is gazing in front of him with a worried expression. Both characters seem engrossed in their own thoughts. It is a moment of waiting. As a matter of fact, Joseph is making a cross; you can spot both crossbars underneath his left foot. The painting evokes Jesus's future death, despite the fact that he is portrayed at such a young age. Joseph seems to be already aware of what awaits Jesus; these elements are what give the scene such gravity.

## ✳ Where does the painting come from?

We don't know. It was given to the Louvre in 1948, but we do not have any information about its origins. Although George de La Tour was very famous in his lifetime, he was gradually forgotten after his death. His works were only rediscovered at the beginning of the 20th century. Today this painting is one of his most famous works.

## The Peasant Family

Around 1640-1645, oil on canvas, 1.13 x 1.59 m
Louis or Antoine Le Nain (Laon, 1600/1610 – Paris, 1648)
Location: Sully 2nd Floor - Painting (France)

24

## ✳ This is a large family.

There are a lot of children. There are actually six of them, including two who are more difficult to spot, on the left, in the background. They are not playing. They have pensive looks; one of them blows into a flute. The child seated on the floor, to the right, seems to be looking in the painter's direction. A little girl stands behind him. In the back, three others are gathered around the fire.

## ✳ They look poor.

The kids don't have shoes. Some of their clothes have holes and are patched. The room is sparsely furnished, just a table and a few chairs.

## ✳ There are animals!

Yes, there's a cat hiding behind a cooking pot and a small dog sitting in the foreground. It was not unusual to see animals in a peasant's home in the countryside.

## ✳ Are they about to eat?

Despite appearances, this is not sure. There are only a few items on the table, among which two empty terracotta bowls. The table-cloth is not properly laid out and the characters are not seated around the table.

The man is about to cut off a slice from the big round loaf and the woman holds a glass of wine.

## ✳ There is only one glass for everyone.

Not only is there only one glass, but also it is quite an odd one. Peasants didn't use to drink from this type of glass, as they were too fragile and too expensive. Rather, they would use goblets made of terracotta, like the other dishes depicted in the painting. The artist probably intended to highlight the liquid contained in the glass. The wine, which would not be visible in an opaque container, contrasts sharply with the woman's white garment, enhancing it even more.

## ✳ Why is there only bread and wine?

Just like *Christ in the Carpenter's Workshop*, the painting is not a simple genre scene. The bread and the wine are most likely religious symbols. By choosing to represent only bread and wine, the painter recalls Christ's words during the Last Supper, the final meal he had with his disciples. After the crucifixion, wine will become the symbol of his blood, bread, the symbol of his body.

**✳ The characters are completely stiff.**

All the adults are looking in the painter's direction. They seem to be posing for the artist. The young musician marks the painting's main axis, while the two women are placed symmetrically about. This apparent immobility reinforces the gravity of the scene, and suggests that silence reigns in the room.

**✳ It looks like a series of portraits.**

The adults' faces are highly individualized. Each one asserts his or her personality; their features are more or less pronounced in accordance to their age. The old man's expression, gazing at the viewer, is particularly intense. The Le Nain Brothers owned land in the region of Laon. It is thus quite possible that the characters of this painting were inspired by real people.

**✳ Who would buy this kind of painting?**

This is one of the mysteries surrounding this work. No one knows who commissioned it, even though it is quite an ambitious piece— the largest painting made by the Le Nain brothers known. They have taken particular care in the treatment of light—expressing subtle nuances between the glowing red of the fire in the background and the blond light coming from the right, which bathes the characters around the table. The fabrics and the characters' skins were rendered in minute detail as well.

**✳ Did more than one person make this painting?**

This masterpiece was created in the workshop of the three Le Nain brothers—Louis, Antoine and Mathieu. Two of them (Louis and Antoine) most likely participated in its execution. Since the artists signed only with their last name, it is difficult to determine who painted what.

Indeed, it was frequent in the 17th century for artists to gather in a workshop and work under the direction of a better-known master, whose style they would copy. This was the case in Rubens's workshop for instance. The master's assistants sometimes specialized in a particular subject—one would paint the flowers while another would deal with architectural patterns. Some of them would later leave the workshop to take charge of their own team.

**Were the Le Nain brothers appreciated in their lifetime?**

Yes. Collectors liked paintings with a realistic topic. There were even replicas of some of the Le Nains' creations, proof of their success. In those days, the notion of a work's uniqueness was less important. Some copies were created in the workshop where the first version had been produced and some were executed by imitators. It is not always easy today to distinguish the initial version from the copies. The art historians' task is to attempt to analyze the style in order to distinguish the hand that produced the original, as well as to differentiate a workshop's or imitator's painting from the master's work.

**Why do we know so little about these painters?**

Collectors never neglected the production of the Le Nain brothers, even after their death. Yet, if their work and life remain fairly unknown, it is because during the Revolution the religious ensembles they had executed for Laon and for Paris were destroyed.

Ironically, during this contrasted era, the Louvre took in some of the Le Nain's works such as *La Forge*.

It was not until the 19th century that we found out more about their activity, thanks to the works of Champfleury, who wrote several manuscripts about them in 1850 and 1862. As a result, young artists such as Gustave Courbet and Édouard Manet were inspired by the more realistic painters of the 17th century and felt a stronger desire to paint real life instead of myths.

## The Pilgrimage to Cythera

1717, oil on canvas, 1.29 x 1.94 m
Antoine Watteau (Valenciennes, 1684 – Nogent-sur-Marne, 1721)
Location: Sully, 2nd Floor - Painting (France)

25

★ **It looks like a garden party.**
The artist must have been inspired by the parties organized by nobility in the gardens of their countryside châteaux. There's lightness in the air. There are lots of people conversing; they are dressed in bright colors, with fabrics that seem to shine like they were made of silk.

★ **Is this water, behind the characters?**
The artist depicted some sort of an inlet in the background, as if the scene was taking place by the sea. According to mythology, the Greek Island of Cythera was formed as a result of Venus's birth. She is the goddess of love, and the island was dedicated to her. This is why at the time, when you said you were "going to Cythera," it meant that you were going to look for a sweetheart. The statue on the right probably represents the goddess. The characters are about to embark on a ship that you can see on the painting's extreme left. We don't know if they are on their way to the island or if they have already arrived and are preparing to leave.

★ **Some of the characters are flying!**
As a matter of fact, small angels turn in circles above the boat, on the upper left side, thus letting us know that this scene is not reality. Besides, the boat doesn't look real; it resembles a stage set. Apparently, this is a scene from a stage play—the Pilgrimage to Cythera was actually a fashionable theatrical topic at the time. During his life, Watteau frequently worked for the theater and the opera, creating sets and portraits of actors...

★ **The landscape is very important.**
The landscape is no longer in the background, as it was in the *Mona Lisa* for instance, but stretches throughout the entire painting. For the artist, nature was as important as the characters. He studied the effects of mist, the reflections of mountain and sky in the water. He actually studied many of the Northern painters from Flanders (present day Belgium), some of whose work was entirely dedicated to landscape painting.

* **The characters form couples.**

  Yes... Each of the couples is in the midst of a romantic conversation. Three of them, on the hill in the foreground, symbolize three different stages of love—in the first couple, the man is kneeling and whispering something into the woman's ear, a sign of desire; in the second, the man courteously helps the woman to stand up, a sign of complicity; in the third one, the man has his arm around the woman's waist, but she is looking over her shoulder, an obvious sign of regret...

* **What indicates that their conversations are about love?**

  By the first couple's feet is a little boy. We know that he is Cupid, son of Venus, because he is seated on a *quiver* (a case to store the arrows), with his bow hanging onto the statue behind him. It is said that once he has pierced a human's heart with his arrows, the latter will irremediably fall in love. So it seems clear that Cupid is responsible for creating all the couples in the painting.

* **Where did inspiration for such a topic come from?**

  Most likely from Watteau's contemporaries—the plays of Dancourt or Fuzelier or the ballets of Duché and Desmarets, whose setting were often the island of Cythera. Their light topics were extremely successful at the time. You can also find the same themes treated in plays by Marivaux. The term *Fête Galante* refers to a painting whose subject combines reality with myth and describes games of seduction.

* **It is well composed...**

  Watteau placed his characters along diagonal lines that cross the rectangular shape of the canvas. The heads of the third couple in the foreground are just beneath the two diagonals' meeting point. Thus, in spite of the important place that is allotted to the landscape, the artist has managed to highlight his characters, who give us codes to decrypt the painting.

**✳   … but it is not very well painted!**
This is not exactly so… After Watteau's death, the technique he
employed for this painting was much criticized; for in order to
render the reflections and the blurry quality of the landscape, he
used small strokes that become visible when you are close to the
painting. Sometimes the paint is thick, as with the leaves, sometimes it is very transparent, slightly diluted, as with some of the
grassy areas in the foreground. At the end of the 18th century,
people were so used to precise, minute technique and so favored a
slick, glossy rendering, that some painters didn't hesitate to affirm
that the painting was "botched."

**✳   So the painting was not a success?**
On the contrary! In the artist's lifetime, the painting was highly
appreciated. The artist had painted it with the aim of being accepted
by the Academy—the artists' official organization. In spite of the
subject's novel character and technique, the painting received the
approval of the venerable institution's members, who were in
general not very indulgent. Watteau's example will be followed by
artists who would specialize in the *Fête Galante* theme, to the great
pleasure of the era's collectors.

**✳   Who would buy this kind of painting?**
In general, this type of painting was commissioned by members of
the nobility or upper middle classes. They enjoyed decorating their
mansions with lighter topics than the traditional antique or biblical
history themes. Painting was no longer a subject of contemplation in
and of itself, but was becoming part of a dwelling's general decor.

# The Skate

1725-1726, oil on canvas, 1.14 x 1.46 m
Jean-Siméon Chardin (Paris, 1699 – Paris, 1779)
Location: Sully, 2nd Floor - Painting (France)

26

**✱ There's a ghost with his eyes and mouth in the upper-middle part of the painting!**
It's a skate or ray, a funny flat diamond-shaped fish, hanging from a hook. It is difficult to identify, since Chardin painted its underside, hence showing its stomach. What we take for eyes and a mouth are actually its gills. You can also make out other fish (maybe a carp), a cat and oysters...

**✱ The painting is set in a kitchen?**
As a matter of fact, Chardin chose to depict very simple objects—a bowl and a saucepan, a terracotta pot hiding part of a skimmer, a knife and a small spice jar behind the cat.
The ray had obviously just been cut open in order to gut it.

**✱ The cat is about to fall!**
The cat is the only living element in the painting. It seems so alive, that it is almost bristling with anger! What has it seen on the counter top? With its paws on the oysters, it looks like it won't be long till it loses its balance on the pile of shells.

**✱ There are not many colors in this painting.**
Chardin uses the entire range of browns, yellows and reds. The copper utensils are the same color as the wall and the ray. Yet you can't confuse them. The utensils' reflections allow us to identify the various materials that are depicted (flesh, shells, fabric, stone...).

**✱ Is it a real kitchen?**
Chardin often painted objects that belonged to him; we can recognize them from one painting to another. However, here, they are oddly arranged—you would never see a cook place a bowl on its side like that, with a skimmer precariously balanced on top of it. Hanging over the edge of the counter, the knife looks dangerously about to fall.

**✱ Was it Chardin who arranged the objects for this painting?**
Certainly... Here, the elements are arranged by category—the dishes are on the right, while the food is on the left. The ray marks the boundary between the two. The tablecloth was certainly not just thrown into the composition casually. It is folded into the saucepan, to better reveal the fish.

* **Chardin liked to paint objects.**
  Even though he specialized in still-lifes, that is to say the representation of objects or dead animals, Chardin broke the rules by adding a live animal to this composition, even though the latter is not the main subject.

* **Is it easier to paint inanimate objects?**
  This is what was believed at the time. Besides, a still-life was less expensive to buy than a portrait. It was considered that painting an expression or feeling was more complicated and noble than describing a vase, no matter how finely executed it may be. Nevertheless, it is as difficult to render the sticky quality of the ray's skin or the shiny aspect of the copper in contrast to the matte texture of the background wall. In fact, the topic Chardin picked was not as easy to paint as it may have seemed in the first place.

* **How did he render the different textures?**
  He mostly used strokes of different shapes and lengths. For the ray's body, he worked with small brush strokes that are rather visible when you're close to the painting. For the oysters, the strokes are broader and he left color base visible in order to suggest the water in the seashell. He used lighter, almost white, stains in order to render the reflections on the dishes.

* **It's a big painting!**
  It is rather large indeed. Later on, Chardin would more frequently paint tiny, little still-lifes, which were easier to sell. However this painting was important to him. He wanted to show off his talent. He painted this while he was young and unknown. With this work, he was hoping to be recognized.

* **Why didn't he choose to paint more luxurious objects?**
  In fact, Chardin executed two paintings: one features the preparation of goods (*La Raie*) and the other features food on the service buffet in a reception room (*Le Buffet*). Thus, he showed his virtuosity in describing all kinds of materials, from the lowest to the most sophisticated. Chardin submitted both paintings to the Academy on the same day. The purpose was to be accepted in this institution. Indeed, you needed to submit two works: one to be approved, the other to be accepted. Both works are displayed in the Louvre.

**✻ Did people like his painting?**
Yes... Everybody was impressed. Though, at that time, it was rare that a still-life painter would be distinguished. People even believed that a more famous master had actually painted the picture. The members of the Academy were so impressed that they immediately accepted Chardin into their group.

**✻ So Chardin was a famous painter then?**
Yes... He was admired by many including King Louis XV. Many artists have subsequently admired this artwork and come to the Louvre to copy it. Cezanne was one of them. In addition, it's one of the first paintings by this artist to have been displayed at the Louvre. Moreover, it was the study of Chardin's still-lifes that confirmed Édouard Manet's and Paul Cézanne's desire to try another genre, despite the fact that it was considered minor at the time. They were able to contemplate these paintings at the Louvre, where they were displayed in the 19th century thanks, among others to the La Caze legacy.

## *The Marquise de Pompadour*

1775, pastel with gouache highlights on grey-blue paper mounted on canvas; 1.75 x 1.20 m
Maurice Quentin de La Tour (Saint-Quentin, 1704 – idem, 1788)
Location: Sully, 2nd Floor – Prints and French Drawings

27

**✱ This woman is wearing a really nice dress!**
The richness of the fabrics and lace informs us that Madame de Pompadour, King Louis XV's "*favorite*" (his official mistress), is one of the kingdom's important figures. Her dress, despite its ornateness, is not a ball gown but an ordinary Court dress. She wears neither a wig nor jewels and on her feet are simple slippers, indicating that she is portrayed in an intimate setting.

**✱ She doesn't look very comfortably seated.**
In order to create volume, the particularly wide dresses worn by noblewomen of the time were supported by armatures—umbrella-like ribs—called panniers or crinolines. These armatures seriously hampered movement during everyday life; it was thus not easy to sit comfortably. Here, part of the fabric and the pannier lie on the chair's arm—the back of the chair prevents them from being properly arranged behind her.

**✱ Is she in her apartment?**
It's a possibility, but we do not have a sufficiently precise description of the apartment she occupied in the Versailles Palace to be absolutely certain. The landscape painting, inlaid in the blue-green and gold paneling, was a decoration in fashion at the time, just like the carpet on the floor beneath the Marquise's feet.

**✱ This painting is quite large for a portrait!**
Indeed, the painting is almost six feet tall and over four feet wide. The Marquise wished to have a full-length portrait, that is to say a portrait that shows her from head to toe. Much more expensive than head-and-shoulder or mid-sized portraits such as the *Mona Lisa*, this type of framing better suits a ceremonial portrait intended to highlight the model's social ambition. Although the composition suggests a certain intimacy, the work is indeed destined to be shown to the public of the Salon (The Academy art show), and to assert the Marquise's power.

**✱ Was she a musician?**
The music score she is browsing through, as well as the guitar and the other music book placed on the chair behind her, show that she enjoyed singing. She would gladly perform in front of King Louis XV, in operas or in stage plays, for his entertainment. These performances, given in the king's small apartments, accessible to an intimate few, were opportunities for the sovereign to escape the constraints of the etiquette of Court life.

Her numerous talents are symbolized by other objects in the painting. A portfolio at her feet and an engraving from a treatise on fine gem works on the table, suggest that the Marquise practiced these arts.

✳ **There are books too.**
The choice of books, whose titles are deliberately visible, is not very consensual—from left to right you can see Guarini's *Pastor Fido*, Voltaire's *Henriade*, Montesquieu's *Spirit of the Laws*, as well as a volume of the *Encyclopedia*, a publication presided over by Diderot that was regularly censored. Though the first book—displaying a pastoral image of Diana goddess of hunting—seems to recall the king's taste for hunting, the other three allude to philosophers who were little appreciated by the king and the Church (particularly the Jesuits). In this way, the Marquise of Pompadour, taking advantage of the king's trust and tenderness, displays her interests in the ideas claimed by these men of letters (religious tolerance, desire for an enlightened monnarchy, dissemination of knowledge).

✳ **It looks different than the other paintings.**
This is not a painting but a pastel. Pastels are color sticks made up of white clay mixed with pigments, Arabic gum and milk or honey. You can draw with these crayons on sheets of paper, which are later mounted on canvas in order to make it more resistant. Pastels give the piece a slightly powdery surface once the pigments have faded.

✳ **Is it frequent to use a paper support?**
While more fragile, paper is suitable for techniques using water-soluble colors, such as water-color and gouache, applied more or less diluted with a brush. Paper is also a good support for ink, which is applied with a quill for more precise rendering of detail. These techniques make use of the paper's color and luminosity, which is never completely covered, unlike with pastels which usually mask the entire underlying support. Nevertheless, these techniques are generally used for studies rather than for finished works.

**✳ Did Maurice Quentin de La Tour use pastels often?**

Yes, he even specialized in it. In the 18th century, pastels were generally used to enhance sketches; later they were chosen by some artists as their exclusive medium. For example, Chardin used it at the end of his life to execute his self-portraits. These are kept in the Louvre, but only showed intermittently because of their fragility. Indeed, since they are made of a powder particularly difficult to fix, pastels are extremely sensitive to light and to shocks, which is why they are displayed only on rare occasions. The portrait of Madame de Pompadour is considered more resistant thanks to the density of its layers of color. This is an exception, for it is one of the rare pastels permanently displayed in the rooms of the Louvre.

**✳ Is it easy to execute such a large pastel?**

Because of their paper support, pastel paintings are rarely this large. This portrait is made up of several sheets, whose joins you can see in the upper part of the picture. Even though they were most likely assembled together on the canvas support beforehand, the artist was constantly confronted with the junctions of the different layers of paper, which could have harmed the ensemble's unity.

**✳ Did the Marquise pose for the entire painting?**

No... You can observe that the face is made of an unevenly edged fragment. The Marquise only posed for this part of the painting and the artist inlaid it into the final composition. Besides, we know of a few funny anecdotes about the artist's whims during these sessions. As a matter of fact, not only did he express the desire to feel comfortable by removing his wig, shoes and collar, but he also refused any kind of intrusion from a third party during the pose, even the king!

**✳**

**Wasn't it quite daring on Madame de Pompadour's behalf to have herself portrayed this way?**

Besides her role as the king's *"favorite,"* the Marquise attempted to impose herself as an adviser. Her involvement in politics earned her many hostile feelings from the Court's conservative members. This piece not only displays her artistic talents, which amused the sovereign, but also her political ambition. Beyond the pomp and circumstance, this portrait is a veiled manner of defending her prized philosophers' new ideas and an attempt to present them to the king, who was not, however, receptive.

# The Consecration of Emperor Napoleon and the Coronation of Empress Josephine in the Cathedral of Notre-Dame, Paris, 2nd December 1804

On the top, detail. Under, full painting
1806-1807, oil on canvas, 6.21 x 9.79 m
Jacques-Louis David (Paris, 1748 – Brussels, 1825)
Location: Denon, 1st Floor – Painting (France)

* **What are all these people doing?**
They are attending an important event, the coronation of the famous Napoleon and his wife Josephine de Beauharnais. At the time, Napoleon was leading France and preparing to conquer a good part of Europe in the years to come. On the day of his conse-cration, he was given objects symbolizing his power—the crown, the scepter and the hand of justice. On the right, you can see men carrying these objects, some of which can still be seen in the Louvre's Objets d'Art Department. However, the moment actually captured in this painting is Josephine's coronation.

* **Where is Napoleon?**
He is the man standing, in profile, on top of the stairs; his crimson garment identifies him. This color has been used to symbolize imperial power since antiquity. Napoleon seems to dominate everyone. In reality he was rather short, so the painter placed him standing next to people who are mostly sitting or placed further down on the steps. Presenting him in a higher position than the rest of the group was an excellent way of conveying the idea that he was in charge.

* **Why does he hold up his arms?**
He is holding a crown that he is preparing to place on the head of his wife, who is kneeling in front of him. She is dressed like him with a crimson coat, specially made for the occasion.

* **Where does the scene take place?**
The coronation took place in Paris, at Notre-Dame Cathedral. It is hard to recognize it, for on this particular day, the choir area was covered with decorative panels that concealed the gothic vaults. However, on the right, you can recognize the sculpture by Nicolas Coustou (Guillaume Coustou's brother, the artist who created the *Marly Horses*)—a Pietà, which is still in the church today.

* **Wasn't an emperor supposed to be crowned in Rome?**
It was indeed the Pope who customarily crowned emperors. But Napoleon forced him to come to Paris for the consecration. Seated behind the Emperor, performing a gesture of benediction, Pope Pius VII doesn't look too happy. On top of forcing him to come to Paris, and in contrast with tradition, Napoleon had auto-pro-claimed himself emperor and then crowned himself, reducing the Pope's importance to that of a mere onlooker.

✳ **You can see all the characters' features.**
This is a real strong point, for you can identify each and every one of the painted characters. Besides, once you've gotten past the first impression of a dense crowd, you realize that each group is clearly distributed and identified. Members of the clergy are behind Napoleon (the Cardinal Caprara on the Pope's right), and officers are in the center (Murat carries a cushion). The imperial family is on the left side of the picture, featuring a little boy dressed in red, holding his mother's hand. His mother is Hortense de Beauharnais, daughter of the Empress—which makes the little boy Josephine's grandson, Prince Napoleon-Charles Bonaparte. In spite of her youthful appearance in this portrait, Josephine was already a grandmother!

✳ **You can almost feel of the coat's velvet.**
In this painting, the artist took particular care in the rendering of fabrics. His technique is precise and he detailed the clothes ornaments as well as the jewels. For instance, you can recognize Josephine's earrings, one of which is displayed today in the Louvre's Galerie d'Apollon.

✳ **Who is the woman sitting in the middle on the rostrum?**
This is Laetitia, the Emperor's mother, even though she actually didn't attend the ceremony, because she had had a fight with her son. But this painting is not designed to depict the reality of the relationships between the various members of the imperial family. On the contrary, it is a propaganda tool and was supposed to give an idyllic vision of them. The painting offers an image of union and power. So it was out of the question to let the public wonder why the Emperor's mother was not present.

✳ **Did David paint the picture alone?**
No. He conceived the composition and executed the most difficult parts, particularly the portraits. But, a painter who specialized in the representation of perspective, Degotti, helped him to complete it. David was at the head of a large studio where several artists worked under his command. Some of them were his students, who came to practice with one of the most famous masters of the day.

## ✳ How do you paint such a large painting?

First, he had to make several series of drawings, in order to determine the emplacement and the composition of the different groups. Then came the sketches, miniature versions of the painting, that allowed choosing colors and lighting. Finally, detailed drawings of the faces were made. It is quite amusing to know that David, a perfectionist, first painted his characters naked in order to better apprehend the movement of their muscles. Thus, a drawing of a naked Napoleon placing the crown on his own head preceded the picture of an imposing and dominating character crowning Josephine. The studies were then submitted to the commissioner, who might ask for alterations. Napoleon asked David to modify the Pope's position—Pius VII is now making a gesture of benediction, when, initially, he had both hands on his knees.

## ✳ The heroes are well centered!

This is a piece that was intended to show the strength and power of the imperial couple. The viewer's eyes had to focus on them. The colors of their garments, their isolation from the rest of the crowd, their position in the central third of the painting—all this helps to set them apart from the rest of the participants. Napoleon, in profile, crowned with laurels, could very well recall a roman emperor. The painting is here to serve the expression of one man's ambition...

## *The Raft of the Medusa*

1818-1819, oil on canvas, 4.91 X 7.16 m
Théodore Géricault (Rouen, 1781 - Paris, 1824)
Location: Denon, 1st Floor – Painting (France)

29

* **It is going to rain—the sky is all black, the waves are huge, the men must be cold!**
By their destitution, the artist shows us that these men have lost everything. Their boat, the *Medusa*, has sunk. They took refuge on a raft made from the boat's remnants. They were not able to take anything with them. Their clothes were probably ripped off during the wreck.

* **Why didn't they use lifeboats?**
There were not enough of them for all the passengers aboard the *Medusa*. This is why they made a raft.

* **Is it a true story?**
It actually is. Everyone was talking about it at the time. There were 149 passengers in the beginning. The survivors remained 15 long days aboard this makeshift raft, without food or drink, before a passing boat rescued them. Many of them died of exhaustion before arrival in France. The ones who survived described the revolt that took place the second day amongst some desperate passengers. On the third day, the most famished ones devoured the bodies of their companions who had died the day before. Injured and starving, some of the survivors lost their minds. Two of the fifteen survivors, Corréard and Savigny, wrote a report about these events, which was published by the press.

* **Was the painter aboard the raft?**
No... Like his contemporaries, he learned about this drama—which had quite moved the public opinion—through the newspapers. He was so interested in the subject that he dedicated several months of his life to it. It has been said that he isolated himself in order to be able to dedicate all his time to the conception of this work. He met with one of the survivors, and he is also said to have recreated a model of the raft to better grasp the horror lived by the shipwrecked castaways.

* **This is not exactly a cheerful theme!**
In the foreground, the very pale men you see are already dead. In order to make them look as realistic as possible, Géricault studied real corpses.
Yet, even though the topic itself is dramatic, the scene Géricault chose to paint bears hope. It is the moment when the survivors see, in the distance, the sail of the boat that is about to save them.

**✹ How does the painter show hope?**

The construction of the painting materializes the rising hope. The men are arranged along a long diagonal starting in the lower left corner and ending in the upper right corner of the canvas. In the foreground, the dead, then the desperate; in the middle of the raft, kneeling men trying to wave; in the background, a man standing on a barrel to wave a piece of cloth and signal the presence of the raft to the approaching boat.

**✹ Where is the boat that is going to save them?**

Far off on the horizon, you can make out a tiny little triangle representing the *Argus*, the boat which would make a detour to rescue them.

**✹ The elements are against them.**

As a matter of fact, there is a wave about to fall on the raft and the wind is pushing the craft in the wrong direction, if you consider the position of the sail. The artist is showing us the fight led by these men against nature, both violent and hostile. This creates additional tension in the painting.

**✹ The dead man in the foreground is only wearing socks!**

The pose and accessories were sometimes a bit artificial, but they are similar the ones studied by painters in the workshops. Thus, the artist shows us how well he knew the governing rules of painting of the times, even though he was undertaking a less academic subject.

**✹ Why did he paint some of the characters only partly?**

He wanted to create an intimacy with the viewer and this type of framing allowed him to give the impression that he was among the shipwrecked and had fallen out of the raft. It was important for Géricault to generate an emotional and affective approach of the event.

**✹ Was the painting well received?**

Not really. It was so unusual to represent a news item, with so many corpses and painted with such realistic colors, on such a big canvas. Pieces of this size were generally reserved for the representation of idealized historical figures, living or dead.

**✳ Is this some kind of painted news report?**

Be careful, news item doesn't mean serious reporting of news— Géricault delivers here his personal interpretation of the drama. It is not something he transcribed on the spot, as would a television crew, reporting live about a tanker wreck or a serious road accident. The topic is most of all a pretext to show the men's distress and the violence of the world.

**✳ Why paint such a painting when the topic was likely to shock?**

For Géricault, heroes did not have to be embodied by historical characters (such as kings or Napoleon), or legendary ones (such as Hercules or Venus). Simple men going through extraordinary events were heroes too. Their experience was as thought provoking as any other historical event. Today, without this painting, we all would probably have forgotten about the *Medusa*. The painting contributed to the infamy of this shipwreck.

**✳ To whom did he intend to sell the painting?**

On account of its size, he would not have been able to sell the painting easily to a private collector. It is furthermore not that pleasant to live with such a tragic picture under your gaze everyday. It was destined rather for a museum or a public setting... and it was actually acquired by the Louvre in November 1824, a few months after the artist's death.

**✳ So he never knew that his painting was going to hang in the Louvre one day?**

In fact he had presented it during his lifetime at an exhibition, the Salon, which was held at the Louvre. The museum didn't purchase it at the time and the painter had to do with a gold medal as compensation for his expenses. He died very young, at the age of 32, of illness. So, sadly, he never knew that his work would become one of the museum's most famous pieces.

*Liberty Guiding the People, 28<sup>th</sup> July 1830*

1831, oil on canvas, 2.60 x 3.25 m
Eugène Delacroix (Charenton-Saint-Maurice, 1798 – Paris 1863)
Location: Denon, 1st Floor – Painting (France)

30

* **There's a big cloud.**
  This is actually smoke that is mixed with the clouds in the background, as happens when there is a fire. This is the way the artist conveys the confusion and turmoil that reign in the scene.

* **There are characters standing, walking on a building's ruins.**
  This is a barricade, that is to say a sort of makeshift barrier made up of stones, cobblestones and debris. Like a huge shield, a barricade serves to block a street and to protect fighters from the gunshot coming from the opposite camp during a street battle.

* **It looks like war.**
  There are, as a matter of fact, dead people pictured in the foreground; others, ready to fight, are brandishing weapons. There's even an armed child. We have the feeling that they are about to step over the dead. With this painting, Delacroix related his vision of the revolution that took place in Paris in 1830. The artist had witnessed these events.

* **Why depict a child?**
  Poor children, left to their own devices, participated in the 1830 revolution. The theme of the fighting children would later inspire Victor Hugo to create his character Gavroche, in *Les Miserables*, in 1862. It is quite possible that Delacroix's painting could have inspired Hugo when he imagined Gavroche's death on a barricade.

* **Why are these people revolting?**
  The French people took to the streets to shout their anger and fight against King Charles X's troops, for the king, amongst others, had refused to use the red, white and blue flag chosen by the people during the 1789 Revolution. This flag symbolizes freedom and equality between men. But it reminded the King of the events during which his family had been chased from the throne and his brother Louis XVI had been executed.

✳ **The flag is the central element of the painting.**
The painting is composed in such a way as to highlight the flag. It is situated in the best section, with its bright red standing out against the clouds. Part of the flag is at the top of a triangle whose left side is formed by the back of the crawling man and the rifle of the one wearing a tube-shaped hat; the triangle's right side is suggested by the line connecting the two guns in the child's hands; as for its base, it is made up of the two corpses in the foreground.

✳ **It looks like the woman is the leader.**
That's right. The only woman in the scene dominates it completely. She is the one carrying the flag. She's leading everyone forward and looks over her shoulder as if to encourage them.

✳ **Why are her breasts bared?**
With this odd bit of nudity, the painter makes us understand that, unlike the other protagonists in the painting, she is not a real woman. She represents an idea, an allegory, just like the naked women in Titian's *Concert Champêtre*.

✳ **What does she represent?**
This woman evokes the French Republic. For a long time, it was customary to use the effigy of the king to symbolize the country, particularly on medals. After the 1789 revolution and the destitution of royal power, this had to be changed in France. It was decided that the country would now be represented by a woman wearing the Phrygian cap (like the one she wears in the painting). This emblem was adopted by the *sans-culottes* (the name given to the radical French Republicans) in 1789. The origins of this choice remain obscure—the Phrygian cap was known to be the cap worn by the inhabitants of Phrygia (a Greek province located in Asia Minor), but it was also thought to be the symbol of the emancipated slaves during antiquity. Thus it represented freedom. The woman thus not only symbolizes France, but also France as the country of Liberty.

✳ **You can see towers in the distance on the right.**
These are the towers of Notre-Dame Cathedral in Paris. At the time, this was one of the tallest buildings in the city. The revolutionaries had succeeded in putting up a red, white and blue flag on top of one of the towers, to prove their strength and determination. If you take a closer look, you can actually see it in the painting. Had these events taken place a few years later, they would probably have chosen the Eiffel Tower ...

* **Was Delacroix a revolutionary?**
Delacroix was in Paris during the Revolution; he was in charge—like several other painters—of looking after the collections of the Louvre. He attended the events without taking part in them and attested to this with this piece. Many other contemporary artists would be inspired by the 1830 revolution, but the only painting that became famous was Delacroix's, most probably because it perfectly summed up the reasons and hopes of this revolution. The painting is still for many people today a representation of Liberty and the Republic.

* **Did people like the painting?**
Not everybody liked it. The public found the woman vulgar and didn't understand the combination of reality and allegory. But it satisfied Louis-Philippe, who was carried to the throne by this revolution. He authorized the Ministry of the Interior to buy the painting for the national collections. Because of its topic, they didn't dare display it permanently at the Luxembourg Museum, even though, at the time, its walls were reserved for works from living artists. But his didn't keep Delacroix from having a brilliant career. He was later commissioned to decorate the Galerie d'Apollon at the Louvre.

# *Chartres Cathedral*

1830,retouched in 1872, oil on canvas, 0.61 x 0.51 m
Camille Corot (Paris, 1796 – *idem*, 1875)
Location: Sully 2$^{nd}$ Floor, Painting (France)

31

### The light is bright despite the clouds.

The sun illuminates the cathedral's main façade. It is probably mid-day, when the light is the brightest, for there is hardly a shadow around the figures, and the one on the wall on the cathedral side is quite short. The path, painted in yellow ochre, enhances the impression of brightness. Corot was certainly very interested in the variations of light on all these shades of beige.

### The characters are not very detailed.

The silhouettes are simply suggested with a few colored spots. On the one hand, they bring life to the composition, which would be rather inert without them; and on the other hand, the characters' proportions also serve to give an idea of the distances separating the different elements of the painting, and the scale of the monument. Without being the main subject of the composition, they contribute to the creation of perspective.

### Did Corot reproduce the monument faithfully?

He took much care in depicting the cathedral's architectural details—the *rosace* (the circular or "rose" window situated between the two church towers), the buttresses (the exterior pillars supporting the cathedral's vaults)...

On the other hand, it is difficult to recognize the building's urban environment—two mounds on the right are hiding the biggest part of the city. As a result, we get the impression that the scene is actually taking place in a village. Corot used the trees planted on these two mounds as a visual echo of the two steeples on the church.

### Did Corot travel a lot?

Yes... Specializing in landscapes, as Theodore Rousseau or Paul Huet, he often traveled in order to discover new sites, which would become the themes for his painting. For this reason, he traveled several times to Italy, Switzerland and various French regions which offered him urban or rural motifs.

In past centuries, nature was considered a mere background decor for a historical or mythological scene, as is the case for *Mona Lisa* or *Concert Champêtre*. In the 19th century though, a wild landscape, urban or rural, became a full-fledged theme for painters. Following in Corot's footsteps, a great number of artists were going to dedicate themselves almost exclusively to landscapes. This was the case for Daubigny, and later for Monet, Sisley...

### Why choose to paint a cathedral?

Built in the beginning of the 13<sup>th</sup> century, around the same time as the Louvre fortress, the Chartres Cathedral was, and still is, a very important monument of Gothic architecture. This style of architecture was blossoming in the Middle Ages, a time when Chartres had known great intellectual influence. The Middle Ages had been ignored for a long time, for they were considered an obscure era. In the 19<sup>th</sup> century, though, they suddenly became the subject of a craze. Some examples attesting to this—the novel *Notre-Dame de Paris* that Victor Hugo wrote the same year Corot was painting this *Chartres*.

In addition, a commission was created, whose concern was to make an inventory of the national historical monuments—including cathedrals—as well as to restore and to preserve them. It was called the Commission des Monuments Historiques (Historical Monuments Commission), and Prosper Mérimée was one of its inspectors. People began to take into account not only their historical value but also their aesthetic one.

### Isn't it difficult to paint such a complex monument, architecturally speaking?

As a matter of fact, a cathedral includes a great many architectural elements (openings, buttresses, pinnacles...) making the task rather arduous. These elements multiply the effects of light and shadow, which are the main preoccupation of a landscape painter.

### So Corot was not painting his final canvases outside?

No... It was rare in 1830 to see someone paint a picture on location. Landscape painters would often study their theme first, executing oil, watercolor or pencil studies on location. Watercolor was particularly appreciated by English landscape painters such as Bonington or Turner. It allowed them to work quickly. It was also easier to handle than oil, which took longer to dry, and whose packaging made of pigskin made it more bothersome to use outdoors in open air. Once their studies were executed, the painters would recreate the landscape, altering it slightly for composition purposes. The result obtained was not a faithful replica of the initially observed theme. The artist did not intend to sell these studies; they were kept and used as a sort of catalogue of shapes and colors.

### Was this painting just a study for the painter?

It is actually possible that Corot first considered this painting as a simple study. Indeed the canvas is not very large; he could have painted it in front of the Cathedral. Many of his small size works—presented in museums today as if they were finished—are actually originally studies. Moreover, Corot never exhibited *Chartres Cathedral* in his lifetime.

* **If Corot only intended to execute a study, does that mean that he didn't consider this painting a major work?**
It is not that simple! Corot had given this painting to an unknown third party; it was returned to Corot in 1871, with seriously damaged edges. From what his friends related, Corot was extremely angry and decided to not only restore it but also to alter it. He added the small character sitting on the stone on the left, as well as the shadow cast in the foreground. This would have been going through a lot of trouble for a mere study!

* **Can you say that Corot was a precursor to landscape painting?**
To paint landscapes or to paint on location meant that the final painting would be executed outside. This is not the technique generally used by Corot, who favored studio work.
However, Etienne Moreau-Nélaton, a collector who owned this painting, considered Corot as a precursor to Claude Monet, Alfred Sisley or Berthe Morisot. These artists would attempt, with some difficulty, to promote outdoor painting, more faithful in rendering the effects of light. They would sometimes paint series showing the variations of light from hour to hour, as did Monet with his series "The Rouen Cathedrals." With this apparently more basic technique, they were hoping to retrieve a spontaneity that was lacking in the studio work. The sketchy quality of one of Monet's works called "Impression, Sunrise," will earn them the nickname *Impressionists* given to them by a journalist hardly appreciative of these new techniques.

* **Did Corot know the Impressionists?**
Yes. He knew the first ten years of their activity. He was actually Berthe Morisot's teacher. As for Sisley, he presented himself at the Salon (The Academy Art Show) as a student of the old landscape artist. If the Impressionists didn't hesitate to assert their indebtedness to Corot, there's a possibility on the other hand that *Chartres Cathedral* had evolved under their influence. This would explain the care he took in restoring and completing in 1871 a painting executed in 1830 and which he may have first considered a simple study.

# Chronology of the works

# Useful tips

# Appendix

Location of the works in the museum

Find out more

# Chronology of the works

The different colors correspond to the those used for localizing the works in each of the museum's different wings:

| Denon | Sully | Richelieu |
|---|---|---|

Despite their dating, the works by Caravaggio are displayed in the 17th century section. Indeed, the artist's works mark a break with Renaissance art and herald the arrival of "Caravaggism," one of the major artistic movements of the 17th century.

# Location of the works
# in the museum

| DENON | SULLY | RICHELIEU |
|---|---|---|
| **MEZZANINE** | | |
| | | *Winged Assyrian Bulls.*<br>Oriental Antiquities Department |
| | | *Basin* known as the *Baptistère of Saint Louis*,<br>Muhammad ibn al-Zayn.<br>Islamic Arts Department |
| | | *Milo of Croton*, Pierre Puget.<br>Sculpture Department (France), Cour Puget |
| | | *Marly Horses*, Guillaume Coustou.<br>Sculpture Department (French section),<br>Cour Marly. |
| **GROUND FLOOR** | | |
| *Slaves*, Michelangelo<br>Sculpture Department (Italy) | *Aphrodite*, known as *Venus de Milo*.<br>Greek, Etruscan and Roman Antiquities Department | |
| **1ST FLOOR** | | |
| *The Winged Victory of Samothrace*<br>Greek, Etruscan and Roman Antiquities<br>Department, Daru staircase | *The Seated Scribe*.<br>Department of Egyptian Antiquities | *Virgin and Child from the Sainte Chapelle*.<br>Objets d'Art Department |
| *Saint Francis of Assisi Receiving the Stigmata*,<br>Giotto di Bondone.<br>Painting Department (Italy), Salon carré | **2ND FLOOR** | |
| *Mona Lisa*, Leonardo da Vinci.<br>Painting Department (Italy) | *Christ in the Carpenter's Shop*,<br>Georges de la Tour.<br>Painting Department (France),<br>Georges de La Tour | *The Madonna of Chancellor Rolin*, Jan Van Eyck.<br>Painting Department (Flanders) |
| *Concert Champêtre*, Titian.<br>Painting Department (Italy) | *The Peasant Family*, Louis or Antoine Le Nain.<br>Painting Department (France) | *The Ship of Fools*, Hieronymus Bosch.<br>Painting Department (Flanders) |
| *The Wedding Feast at Cana*, Veronese.<br>Painting Department (Italy) | *The Pilgrimage to Cythera*, Antoine Watteau.<br>Painting Department (France) | *Self-Portrait*, Albrecht Dürer.<br>Painting Department (Germany) |
| *The Fortune-Teller*, Caravaggio.<br>Painting Department (Italy),<br>Grande Galerie | *The Skate*, Jean-Siméon Chardin.<br>Painting Department (France) | *The Meeting at Lyon*, Peter Paul Rubens.<br>Painting Department (Flanders) |
| *The Consecration of Emperor Napoleon<br>and the Coronation of Empress Josephine*,<br>Jacques Louis David.<br>Painting Department (France) | *The Marquise de Pompadour*,<br>Maurice Quentin de La Tour.<br>Graphic Arts Department | *Bathsheba*, Rembrandt.<br>Painting Department (Holland) |
| *The Raft of the Medusa*, Theodore Gericault.<br>Painting Department (France) | *Chartres Cathedral*, Camille Corot.<br>Painting Department (France) | *The Astronomer*, Jan Vermeer.<br>Painting Department (Holland) |
| *Liberty Guiding the People, 28ᵗʰ July 1830*,<br>Eugène Delacroix.<br>Painting Department (France) | | *The Villeneuve-lès-Avignon Pietà*,<br>Enguerrand Quarton.<br>Painting Department (France) |
| | | *Francis I, King of France*,<br>Jean Clouet.<br>Painting Department (France) |

The three different wings of the museum do not have the same number of floors.
Be careful, the works displayed on the same floor, but in two different wings, can be very far apart from one another!

# Useful

# tips

## Louvre info:

Rue de Rivoli
75001 Paris
Welcome Line: 01 40 20 53 17
Website: www.louvre.fr
Metro station: Palais-Royal Musée du Louvre, via line 1 or line 7
Buses: 21, 24, 39, 69, 72, 74, 76, 95

## Is the Louvre open everyday?

• The museum is closed every Tuesday, in order to do a thorough
cleaning of all the rooms.
• It can also be closed on some bank holidays; it is therefore advisable
to check beforehand.
• The Louvre is open from 9 am to 6 pm, except for Wednesdays
and Fridays where you are welcome until 10 pm.
• Be careful, not all rooms are open everyday! A schedule of the room
openings is at your disposal on the Louvre's website. This said,
last minute changes are always a possibility...

## Where are the museum's accesses located?

• There are alternative entrances to the famous **Pyramid**.
One is located at the **Porte des Lions** (The Lions Gate), in the Pavillon
de Flore—on your left when you have your back to the Pyramid,
near the Arc du Carrousel (The Carrousel Arch). The Porte des Lions'
entrance is not open everyday.

• Another access to the Pyramid from the **Passage Richelieu** is reserved for visitors who have already purchased their tickets. This entrance is found when coming out of the Metro-station Louvre-Palais-Royal.
• From the **Metro station: Louvre-Palais-Royal**, you will have direct access to the Carrousel du Louvre's shopping gallery. Here you will also find an underground entrance to the museum.

## How to avoid lines?

• By buying a ticket or a Museum Pass in advance. A pass can be worthwhile if you are counting on making several visits. Remember that children under 18 enter for free. (Presentation of an ID card may be required for the older ones).

## Where can you buy a ticket or a pass in advance?

### For a single visit:
• You can buy a ticket in advance, good for a one-day visit, in the following stores: Fnac, Carrefour, Continent, Leclerc, Auchan, Extrapole, Le Bon Marché, Printemps, Galeries Lafayette, BHV, Samaritaine, Virgin Megastore.
• Passes combining a transportation ticket and a museum entrance ticket are available from the SNCF and the RATP. These tickets are good for museum access as well as for transportation on the Metro and Transilien (Ile-de-France) mass-transit networks.
• The Carte "Musées et Monuments" (Museum and Monuments Pass) is valid for 1 to 5 days and gives you instant access to numerous Parisian touristic sites. It is on sale at the different monuments, in Metro stations as well as at the City of Paris's Tourist Bureau.

### For the those who visit the Louvre several times a year:
• The Carte des Amis du Louvre (Friends of the Louvre Card) is for sale in the office of the association with the same name. It is located underneath the Pyramid and is a good solution for the inhabitants of the Ile-de-France (Paris area). It also gives access to the exhibits held just underneath the Pyramid.
• The museum also offers various types of season tickets for students, artists and teachers.

## How to benefit from free entrance or discounts?

• The Louvre is free for children under eighteen, unemployed persons, welfare recipients with proper identification and official documents, the disabled, artists affiliated with the Maison des Artistes or the Association Internationale des Arts Plastiques, and art teachers.
• On Friday nights after 6 pm, entrance is free for those under 26, while others benefit from half-price tickets.

## Can you see everything with a single ticket?

• One single ticket gives access to all the departments and it is valid, all day, until closing time. You can thus enter and exit as often as you like on the same day. You must keep your ticket in order to present it to museum controllers if necessary.
• Unlike the exhibitions that take place among the actual collections of the Louvre, which are accessible with the museum ticket, the temporary exhibitions organized underneath the Pyramid are subject to special admission rates.

## Is food available in the museum?

• Inside the museum itself, there are two cafés: one is installed in the Denon wing and the other in the Richelieu wing. There is also a café, a self-service and a full-service restaurant situated beneath the Pyramid. You can also have lunch at the Restorama, which is a group of cafeterias, proposing food from various countries around the world. Located in the Galerie du Carrousel, underground, it is quite crowded and noisy, but it is also quite inexpensive and children enjoy the fast-food style.
• Don't forget the Jardin des Tuileries or the Jardins du Palais-Royal, just outside the Pyramid, where you can have picnics and play games, which is a nice playful way of concluding your visit to the Louvre.

# Find out more

• **Information cards, written by the museum's scientific crew, are at your disposal in each of the display rooms.** They will allow you to complete the information you will find in this book. But be careful, their content is sometimes quite specialized and, therefore, not particularly adapted to children.

• **Françoise Barbe-Gall,** *How to Talk to Children about Art*, Frances Lincoln, 2005, 184 p.

• **Geneviève Pierrat-Bonnefois,** *Egypt at the Louvre, a Guided Tour*, "Chercheur d'Art", RMN, Paris, 1998, 40 p.

• **Serge Prigent,** *The Louvre, Dates, Facts and Figures*, Jean-Paul Gisserot, 2004, 63 p.

• **Audioguides** available at the Richelieu, Sully and Denon entrances.

• **www.louvre.fr**
Here you will find all the necessary information regarding the museum and most notably what you will need to prepare a visit:
- The "œuvres" menu offers short introductions about each department, as well as maps and a selection of commented works.
- The "Atlas" menu gives access to a database of the works presented in the museum. This can be useful to prepare a tour based on a theme or an artist.

**Photographic credits :**

© AKG-images : cover & p. 8, 15, 26-27, 40-41, 56, 68, 84, 120, 132, 148, 156, 160, 164. Photos Erich Lessing : p. 16-17, 44, 48, 60, 68, 72, 80, 88, 92, 96, 100, 104, 108, 112, 116, 124, 128, 136, 140, 144, 152.
© RMN p. 40-41, 64. Photo R.G. Ojeda : p. 76, G. Blot/C. Jean : p. 52.

Drawing of the back cover and the title page:
**José Bulnes**

Publishing director:
**Laurence Golstenne**
assisted by **Hélène Lévy**
Design and layout:
**Robaglia Design**
Copy-editor:
**J. Liesveld**

Photoengraved and printed September 2005
by the printer **Groupe Horizon**
**Parc d'activités de la plaine de Jouques**
**200, avenue de Coulin**
**13420 Gémenos, France**